Aspire to Inspire: Stories of Hope & Renewal

Inspirational Short Stories about struggles, sufferings, challenges and victories.

Letty Ramirez
Henry Trevino

Copyright © 2020 Letty Ramirez and Henry Trevino
ISBN-13 978-0-9897820-9-8
ISBN-10 0-9897820-9-3

Cover Art by Sara Edgington

All Rights Reserved. No part of this book may be used or reproduced, in any manner whatsoever, without the written permission of the Author and Publisher.

Printed in the United States of America by Lightening Source, Int'l and distributed by Ingram.

Published by
Watercress Press
14080 Nacogdoches Rd #582
San Antonio, Texas, 78247
www.watercresspress.com

Dedication

This book is dedicated to people who enjoy reading inspirational short stories and to all who opened their heart to share a personal story in hopes of inspiring others.

Introduction

How many times have you heard someone say, *"I could write a book about my life."* Perhaps you have even said it yourself. Well it's true. There is a book inside all of us. This book called *"life"* consists of one's own journey through different experiences that change us, teach us lessons, and strengthen our faith in God. My wish while writing this book, co-authored with Henry Trevino, is a way for others to share something about themselves in hopes of inspiring others. By sharing stories with others, especially when one is going through something similar, there seems to be an automatic connection. We may not change the world, but even if one person is helped by another persons' story, it will be well worth the effort.

I was inspired to write my first book *Traveling Blind*, after the death of my late husband by suicide. Surviving a loved one's suicide was the hardest thing I have ever had to go through. I wrote it to help others who have experienced this kind of pain as a way to express and share how I got to the point of loving life again, and to open my heart to love again. I give full glory to God for never leaving my side, comforting me and ultimately saving me. As I look back now it's hard to see how I made it from point A to point B, not only in my daily life, but also as the weeks, months and years that followed. I realized that my daily journal writing helped to heal me, by evidence that when going back to read my entries, I never remembered writing my own written words. It gave me no choice but to relive the experiences and come to accept that life does go on.

As a way to give back to others for all the love and support I received during my most trying times, I was led to write other peoples' stories in hopes that their words would make it into the hands of those who need them the most. Family members, friends, and even people I didn't know offered to open their hearts and share something in their life that could possibly help someone else with words of encouragement, hope, and an attitude of never giving up.

I have come to the conclusion that the secret to being happy is to pray without ceasing, forgive daily, and be grateful for all the blessings God has placed in my life. I have been on paths that I would never want or choose to travel, but it is with faith that I proceed forward and not question his ways.

There is a purpose for every person who has ever been in my life: some have passed, some have always been a part of my life and some were here for just a little while. I am grateful for all the loves, experiences I've been through, lessons learned and yes even disappointments in my life. They have made me a stronger person with a willingness to help, love and serve others, as I believe that is what God wants.

Letty Ramirez

Table of Contents

A Letter to My Father 1
A Love That Lives Forever 3
A Mothers' Nightmare 7
A Prearranged Coffee Date 14
Amy's Story 18
Around the Bend, Blessings Appear 24
Blessed With a Baby 28
Faith's Story 32
From Rags to Riches 38
God Was Truly My Savior 42
God is Good 45
Hell on Earth 49
It Goes On 52
It Is What It Is 55
Las Vegas Massacre 59
Lest We Forget 64
Living With Anxiety Disorder 68
Love And Devotion 73
Loving Dedication to the End 77
Motherly Love 80
My Battle With Cancer 86
My Dad's Truck 90
My Journey During Dialysis 95
My Life Flashed Before Me 100
My Life's Odyssey 104
My Mother 109
My Sophie 114
Proclamation Of Love 119
Reality Check 123

The Beginning of a Long Career 127
The Circle of Life 131
The Importance of Forgiveness 134
The Power of Prayer 140
The Scar Left Behind 144
Three Months 149
To Love, Only Like a Mother Can 153
Two Loves To Remember – Two Great Women 157
Weeds to Wildflowers – Lessons in Life and Love 162
Unwanted 173
Epilog 178

Letter to My Father

"For God so loved the world that he gave his one and only son, that whoever believes in him shall not perish but have eternal life." John 3:16

Dear Daddy: we are so blessed to have had such a wonderful man in our lives for as long as we did. The many roles you played during your long lifetime have exemplified how we should live our own. Through you wisdom, you taught us many valuable lessons, including those of unconditional love, forgiveness, faith and hope. They will remain engraved in our hearts forever.

You were a World War II veteran, who honorably served your country, yet you were a hero to us in so many other ways. In the eyes of your children and grandchildren, you not only served your country during one of its times of greatest need, but you served God and your family with equal honor.

As a family, we could not keep up with the love that seemed to flow so effortlessly and abundantly from you. You were the center of our family circle by your mere presence and your love for life inspired us. There is no way to measure how grateful and proud we are to have had such a special *"welo"* in the lives of our children. We will always see a part of you in them.

Looking back on the last days of your life, every minute seems to have had significance. Minute by minute, God's perfect and divine plan was being carried out exactly the way it was intended. To witness the death of your earthly body and yet feel you were being resurrected at the same time is something I will never forget. God gave me the courage and the strength I needed to be with you in your last days.

I went from sitting at your bedside and begging you not to leave me, to realizing that you were ready for bigger and better things and I had to let you go. Only a few weeks earlier, you had wanted to return to my house so I wouldn't be alone. You said I needed you; actually, you wanted to take care of me. At 84 years of age, you were still being my dad and wanting to watch over me.

In the last days of your life, you knew you were dying. I witnessed how you went from being somewhat afraid to acceptance and even anticipation, as it appeared that you were catching glimpses of heaven. You talked about the light that was still a little far away. You began talking to your parents and your brother...you wanted to go to mass and talked about what you wanted to wear. You wanted a little time to be alone, and you wanted flowers.

We did everything you asked, Daddy, as we knew that you were preparing yourself for the transition into your new home. Then after spending time with your wife and all your children...you slipped out of our hands and into the loving arms of God's gentle embrace. Immediately after you passed, we witnessed a change in the weather. It poured for a short time and then out came the sun. Perhaps it was your tears of joy, followed by the light signifying that you had arrived at your final destination. Life holds so many mysteries.I know that you are happy and free of any physical suffering, and while we have been left behind, God will continue to comfort us with His everlasting love. – *Letty Ramirez*

Reflection: We grieve for our loss, but we're glad that we had you for so many years. Your dying wish was to be remembered with smiles and laughter rather than tears or anguish. The passing of time will temper the ache in our hearts, and it is then, that we will gladly comply with your dying wish that we remember you with smiles and laughter. – Henry Trevino

A Love That Lives Forever

Jesus said to her, "I am the resurrection and the life. Anyone who believes in me will live, even if they die. And whoever lives by believing in me will never die. John 11:25-26

October 4, 1983, a date etched in my heart; a date never to be forgotten. That was the day that I gave my final farewell to my dear wife who slipped from my arms and wandered into eternal life.

A few months before that fateful day, my wife had been complaining about headaches experienced only in the morning. The headaches disappeared as the day wore on. Many of her girlfriends suggested that they were probably caused by stress, high blood pressure, perhaps experiencing change of life syndrome. She was always careful with her health and always had her yearly physical exams. The results always indicated that she was in perfect health. There were no signs of diabetes, arthritis, high blood pressure, kidney, liver, spleen or pancreas problems.

As the weeks progressed, she would tell me that she had gone to the mall and could not remember where she had parked her car. Again, she went to the family doctor and had a complete physical exam. The doctor showed me her exam results and said that he could not find anything wrong or even suspicious.

As the weeks passed, she never stopped doing her chores around the house; she cooked, cut the lawn, watered the plants, washed our clothes and always kept the house in immaculate condition. We had five children and she tended to each one. She gave them her care and her love and seemed that she could do the impossible in keeping the family on track.

One day I came home from work and found her on the den floor. This was not unusual since she enjoyed lying on the carpeted floor and taking a short nap. This time it was different; she was very lethargic, her speech was slurred and she could hardly keep her eyes open. What little I could understand from her was that she didn't know how she had been able to send Mark, our youngest child to school.

I called my son Mike and asked him to come over and help me check his mother. Mike was a paramedic at the time. He arrived five minutes later. He checked her and said that he could not even venture an opinion on her condition. Mike and I went to the doctor that had just examined her two weeks prior and questioned him about the condition of my wife. Again, he showed us the results of her latest exam. Everything was perfect. I went home but decided to take her to the hospital. I asked Mike to take his younger brother home with him. Mark was just nine years old.

I went to the emergency room and asked for help from the nurses. They took her into an examining room right away. It happened that by chance there was a doctor of neurology at the hospital checking on some other patients. He was called to the emergency room. He told me that she was not his patient; however, he would give her a preliminary exam to see if he could determine her illness. I gave my consent to the doctor. He told me that he was going to give her an MRI and admit her into the hospital. I stayed behind and registered her into the hospital.

After registering her, I went to the waiting room to wait for the doctor. He came to the waiting room and gave me the devastating news that I hoped I would never hear. The doctor told me that my wife had a massive tumor in the back of her head and that it was bleeding into itself. The doctor explained that he was giving her some medication to reduce the swelling and control the bleeding. This was on a Friday. He said that he would operate on her on Monday or perhaps he would have to operate the next day, Saturday.

I went to her room and told her that I was going home to take care of Mark. I also told her that I had given my telephone number to the nurses if she needed to call me. She said goodbye and those were the last words I ever heard her say.

I opened the house door and heard the phone ringing. I was hoping against hope that it was one of my children calling me. How wrong I was; it was the hospital calling for me to go to the hospital because my wife was in very critical condition. Again, I called my son Mike and we both went to the hospital.

I saw the doctor coming towards us with his sleeves rolled up. As soon as he met us, he said, *"I didn't realize how sick your wife was; I don't think she is going to make it."* She had had a respiratory arrest and was now on life support. She lasted in that state for four days. I stood next to her bed for the first thirty-six hours, only leaving her for a couple of minutes at a time.

It broke my heart to see Mark confused and wanting his mother to live. All the nurses got to know him during those few days. He would constantly ask the nurses to check the pump that was keeping his mother alive. He wanted to be sure that the pump was working o.k.

The doctors continued to administer tests to see if there was any brain activity. On the fourth day the doctor finally told us that there was no brain activity and he felt it was hopeless to keep her on life support.

I asked all my sons and daughter to help me make the final decision. They all concurred that they didn't want their mother to continue suffering. Later that day my wife passed away with her mother and father, her sons and daughter and myself around the bed watching her slipping away to go to her final destination.

The greatest impact I had, and that I will never forget was during our last moments with her. When the doctors invited us in to see her for the last time all the apparatus sustaining her life had been removed. She lay in bed covered up to her chest with a clean sheet. She looked very serene with both her hands and arms under the clean sheet.

Marty's father and mother, all the kids and I were around the bed watching her slip away. All of a sudden I saw her right hand come up from under the sheet and go in the direction of her throat. I motioned to a nurse who quickly came and put her hand under the sheet. To this day I still wonder whether she was trying to tell me that she couldn't breathe.

Our lovely mother and wife wandered into an unknown land and left us grieving for her loss. She gave us her loyalty, devotion, dedication, her care and her love. Her life revolved around the health and welfare of her family. She leaves us with loving memories that have been etched into our hearts and will help us remember her till the end of our days. – *Henry Trevino*

Reflections: The love for a mother is one of the most precious gifts that God can bestow on us. When a mother exits into an unknown land, the void left behind is profound and devastating. Memories of loyalty, devotion and dedication, will forever linger in the lives of those she left behind. With her priceless love, her final goodbye words would probably be, "remember me with smiles and laughter for that's the way I'll remember you." – Henry Trevino

A Mothers' Nightmare

Say to those who hearts are afraid, "Be strong and do not fear. Your God will come. He will pay your enemies back. He will come to save you." Isaiah 35:4

It was such a happy time in my life...recently retired after working 32 years with AT&T, our daughter Melissa had recently graduated from Southwest Texas State University and our son Matthew was one month into his sophomore year at Texas A&M. I had so much to look forward to in retirement, lazy mornings drinking coffee, shopping, travel, happy hour with friends. It couldn't get any better.

And then that dreadful day that nobody prepares for. The phone rings at 3AM and it wakes me from a deep sleep. I was alone in our big house, as my husband Dale was in California on business, and I'm so afraid to answer the phone; it can't be anything good. I answer in a panic and I hear my son's, Matthew's voice, *"Mom, I'm in a lot of trouble, I'm in jail and I'm probably going to get kicked out of school."* A mother's nightmare, I'm in disbelief, scared, and don't know what to do. Matthew goes on to tell me that police have gone to his apartment on a tip from someone and have searched and found all kinds of drugs, which mostly belong to him, and they have arrested him.

All I could do was scream and cry in my misery not wanting to believe what Matthew was saying. But then I picture him in a jail cell alone and scared by himself and looking to me to help him. I try to put my misery aside and I tell my son that I will drive to College Station in the morning and that his dad would join us as soon as he can return from his business trip.

I was devastated, alone, and there was no one to console me and tell me all would be ok. After being awakened in the middle of the night I decided I wouldn't do the same thing to Dale especially since he was 1700 miles away. I would let him get a good night's sleep and talk with him the next day. It was a terrible lonely night, unable to sleep and feeling unable to carry the weight of this unexpected situation and I began to pray. *"GOD PLEASE HELP ME GET THROUGH THIS AND PLEASE HELP MATTHEW."*

I decided to call Melissa first so she would know what had happened and that I would be going to College Station. She was shocked and sad but was glad I had let her know. She was worried about Matthew and was also worried about me as I was alone and would be going by myself. I assured her I would be ok and that dad would join me as soon as he could get back. After sleeping a little I got up, got ready and packed a bag. Around 8am (6am in California) I finally called Dale. It was a difficult conversation and having to go through the pain again of what had happened was heart wrenching. Dale was also in disbelief; he was so sorry I had to deal with this while he was out of town. He spoke softly in his attempt to calm me down and he assured me that everything would be fine and that he would book the first possible flight back home and join me.

    I finally headed to College Station. It was a trip that I will never forget. I cried as I drove, and I prayed as my tears streamed down my cheeks. As I reflect on it now, I shouldn't' have made that trip alone. I was too emotional to be driving and totally not safe. But I didn't want to have to tell anyone that our son had been doing drugs and was arrested and now in jail. But I have a strong faith and I know now that during my time of need, God was with me. He was absolutely with me during that long and dangerous drive and He would continue to stay by my side for the next few days while we did what needed to be done to get our son back home.

As I arrived at College Station and looked for the jail, I knew I would have to find a bail bondsman. I knew nothing about these things and the fear of it all was overwhelming. This was nothing I had ever imagined I would have to face. But once again, God provided the necessary strength. After locating the jail, I found a bail bondsman office across the street. And there I met a wonderful young man, an A&M graduate that would help me with this next step that would get me closer to getting my son back. He was kind, warm and easy to talk to and made me feel hopeful. It would take some time to get all the necessary paperwork completed.

The waiting was so difficult and then I would find out that Matthew could not be released until the judge set the bail. In addition, the bail would not be set until the judge met with Matthew. This resulted in another day in jail for Matthew. The delay would create more anxiety for all of us, but it was clearly out of our control.

The next day after discovering that many potential serious charges were involved, Matthew was finally released from jail. It was a very emotional encounter. I was so angry with Matthew for what had led him to jail. Matthew had been doing so well in college, we had been so proud of his high grades. We had no idea of his drug problem; how could this be happening. But I could tell that Matthew's arrest and jail time had scared him and I saw that he was now realizing the seriousness of the matter. I hurt so bad for Matthew and myself, it was a time for crying, but I had my son and my prayers continued.

Matthew and I went to our hotel room and waited for dad. It was a sad and lonesome time. We talked about the seriousness of the situation and I remember Matthew curled up in the bed crying and saying he didn't want to go to prison. My poor young son was so scared, it broke my heart, and I felt completely helpless. But again, feeling God's presence and with all the strength I could muster, I was hopeful and tried to calm my son assuring him we would do all we could to make it all better. Matthew was showing remorse for his actions and I then realized that with God's help we could get through this crisis.

I then realized that we needed to find a lawyer. I remember going through the yellow pages of the College Station directory. There were many to choose from and yet no direction. I did the best I could and again, feeling the presence of God I picked one and made an appointment.

Later that evening Dale finally arrived. I sent Matthew down to meet with his dad for some alone time. It was another difficult and emotional encounter, this time between father and son. Reflecting on all this again confirms that a parent's unconditional love for their children never ceases especially in times of need.

During the course of the next few days many things would happen. Matthew and I would go to the A&M's business office and withdraw him from each of his classes. We would do this before they found out about his arrest. Fortunately, it was early in the semester and a withdrawal rather than an incomplete would appear on his record and financially, we would get a small refund. We had to deal with his apartment. Because he was arrested at his apartment, he could no longer stay there but we had to continue paying rent until it was rented again. The manager understood of the situation and fortunately they were able to rent the apartment within a couple of months, reducing our financial liability.

We finally met with the lawyer. While the lawyer explained that Matthew's charges were very serious, we sensed that the lawyer's experience as a county judge and his knowledge of the law would work favorably for Matthew's circumstances. Once again, we felt God in our presence. He had put us in touch with the best possible lawyer and we were hopeful and grateful. The lawyer explained that when

Matthew's case went to court one of the things that would happen is that the judge would probably order him to a not so favorable state drug and alcohol rehab center. He recommended that to be proactive we should find a rehab center of our choice rather than a state center. If we did this right away while waiting for a court date, it would look favorable in court that Matthew had decided this himself. And that's exactly what we did.

As soon as we got home Dale did some extensive research and found a rehab center close to home in Centerville. He also discovered that as Matthew was still covered under Dale's company medical insurance plan, the cost of the 31-day rehab, which was very costly, would be covered. It was yet another blessing.

Matthew was admitted quickly and during the next 31 days, he would go through a life changing experience. He had his struggles and it was tough for him at first but after maybe a week he was totally committed to the 12-step program. He put his faith as well as his heart and soul into the program and he was on his way to sobriety working the program one day at a time.

Dale and I, and our family and friends mailed Matthew many letters of encouragement, love and support during those 31 days. It was our hope that our heartfelt letters would help Matthew during his time of need. At the end of the 31 days the families of loved ones that were in the rehab center all came together for a deep, emotional experience that would bring us all to tears. There was so much love and support and at the same time pain and fear that would be exchanged amongst ourselves. But it would result in a bonding with our son that would help us to better understand his required commitment to stay sober and our commitment to help him.

During the next year Matthew lived with us and worked hard to successfully live in sobriety. It was a difficult time for him with good days and bad days, but he stayed committed, and during the first 90 days he would do more than 90 AA meetings in 90 days. When he struggled the hardest during those days, he would go to more than one meeting a day. While still waiting for a court date, which would take 8 months, we decided that Matthew should put college on hold for a year and find a job. Dale was able to find him a temporary job at AT&T. The job was a stabilizing force for Matthew, which provided responsibility and order to his life during his recovery time.

Finally, 8 months after the arrest we heard from Matthew's lawyer. He had been able to reduce some of the charges and we were ready to go to court. It would be another emotional time for all of us especially for Matthew not knowing how harsh his punishment would be. The day came and with so much fear and anxiety we appeared before the judge. After the judge reviewed the case, he asked if we had anything to say. Matthew showed remorse and I asked for mercy to please give our son another chance. With that, the judge gave Matthew 5 years of probation and 160 hours of community service with deferred adjudication upon successful completion of his probation. Once again, we knew God was with us. Under the circumstances of the arrest charges, this was the very best we could have hoped for and we were happy.

A year after Matthew's arrest he went back to Texas A&M. Three years later he graduated Cum Laude from Texas A&M. While Matthew was not convicted his arrest is on public records. For several years this made it difficult to find good employment. But Matthew never gave up and for many years he worked hard doing DJ gigs and working after school programs under contract. During this time Dale and I would pray daily with fervor that Matthew be given a chance to find a good job.

St. Mary's Catholic Church was walking distance from Dale's work and for many months Dale would go every day to pray that God answer our prayers and allow our son an opportunity for a meaningful job. Our family has always believed in the power of prayer as well as the will of God. And by the grace of God, Matthew is currently Senior Director of Community Development at the Greater Williamson County YMCA. He works with teens on a variety of programs, some of which he has developed himself, and he is grateful for giving back to the community.

Matthew was arrested in the year 2000 and he was only 19 years of age. As I write this in 2019, Matthew has been sober for 19 years, half of his life. As I recall the devastating memory of the night Matthew called me to tell me he was in a lot of trouble and that he was in jail, it saddens me and brings tears to my eyes. But when I see all the good that resulted from that devastating night, I thank God for saving my son; it brings tears of joy to my eyes. GOD IS GOOD ... ALL THE TIME! – *Elsa Hart*

Reflection: Mothers always carry the heaviest loads of the family. They are always the protectors of their family, especially their children. They will always be your advisor, your confidant, your nurse and the ones that will comfort you when you have a broken heart. Mothers will love you forever. – Henry Trevino

A Prearranged Coffee Date

For we walk by faith, not by sight. - 2 Corinthians 5:7

My husband and I moved from my hometown in Texas to a small town in North Carolina. A job opportunity had come up and we decided it was the best thing to do at the time. I had never lived outside of Texas so it was not easy for me to leave my family and friends behind.

One day while running errands, I came across a women's magazine titled, *Sophie* which caught my eye. I took it home, read it and immediately felt connected. It was a monthly magazine that was delivered to many different businesses all over town. It contained short inspirational stories that I enjoyed reading.

Eventually it got to the point where I looked forward to reading it every month; one would think I was expecting a check in the mail. In every new edition that I received I would read something I needed to hear. I wanted more: more articles, more stories, more inspiration, and more messages from God. I wanted desperately to continue spreading the word of God. When I would go back to Texas to visit, I would pick up a few extra copies for my sisters and asked them to pass them around.

I noticed in one of the monthly issues that Judy, the owner, was considering selling her magazine. My first thought was *"Oh no, please don't do that, I loved that magazine, just the way it was."* My second thought was to email the owner; not that I had any intention to purchase it; I didn't have that kind of money. I just felt that God nudged me in a way that happened so fast; I didn't even have time to think about it. Before I knew it, the send button was pressed, and the email was on its way. I just left it in God's hands. I figured that she probably had already sold it anyway; probably she wouldn't even email me back. But, lo and behold, she did email me back. Just like I thought, she told me that she had already sold the magazine, however she mentioned that she was still going to continue playing a big part in it for a long while.

We emailed a little small talk back and forth and before I knew it we were going to meet for coffee. I don't think either one of us knew why, other than it felt right. We were both very excited after the plans to meet for coffee had been made. We verified the time and place a few days before the meeting. As soon as I saw her, I felt like I had known her all my life. We introduced each other and proceeded to find a table. We talked and talked over coffee like longtime friends do after not seeing each other after a long absence. It was like we picked up from where we left off, only we had never met before. We had some things in common, but the main thing was that we both loved to write.

The miracle about this whole coffee date is that things unfolded in a way that was just not typical. I became friends with the owner and the magazine soon after moving to North Carolina. It became such a part of my spiritual journey that the only explanation of how it got to this point is that God had this prearranged for us. We just didn't have a reason to question it. God had a reason to place that magazine in my path. It led to everything, but it was not an accident; it was on purpose and for a purpose.

About a month after meeting the owner of the magazine I became a contributing writer for that publication. I realized how much I loved reading and writing short stories. It felt good to write personal things I've experienced and hoping someone else might gain something from it just like the other stories did for me.

My husband, Ernie and I made our way back to Texas after about a year; he was offered another job and we wanted to be close to our family. I continued writing for the magazine for several more months. One day unexpectedly, all the contributing writers were notified that the owners were relocating. The future of the magazine was unclear and that all printing would stop for the time being. There would not be any more acceptance of contributing articles.

Although I was disappointed, I was grateful to have been a part of it, even for a relatively short time. I think back to how that coffee date had occurred out of the clear blue; there was no particular intention at the time, yet so much happened because of it. She gave me the opportunity to write for that magazine. We never met in person again, but I gave her a lot of credit because she was definitely a part of the big picture.

My experience in writing stories while in North Carolina brought me back home with that same passion and desire of sharing stories. Perhaps that is one of the reasons God gave me the grace, the ability, and the desire to continue my writing. It was when I got settled back home that the idea of writing this book began to swirl around in my head. I can honestly say that when I pray, I always ask God to place people and situations in my path that will continue to guide me and reveal what it is that He would have me do for him with the talents and gifts he has blessed me with. I firmly believe that that is the reason why sometimes people come into my life, seemingly out of nowhere, and sometimes just in passing; but always for a reason.

I still think back sometimes and wonder about all the things that I would have missed if I had never reached out to her on that one day that came out of nowhere. I believe that God led me during that time. I might not have understood *"why,"* at the time, but it all makes sense to me now. – *Letty Ramirez*

Reflection: Sometimes events, ideas, concepts and spurts of energy will enter our minds and swirl around in our head for days, never knowing how or why. The only logical assumption that can be made is that God had something to do with it. You can assume that God wanted you to do something about what He put in your head. – Henry Trevino

Amy's Story

Despite all these things, overwhelming victory is ours through Christ. And I am convinced that nothing can ever separate us from God's love. Neither death nor life, neither angels nor demons, neither our fears for today nor our worries about tomorrow- not even the powers of hell can separate us from the love of God that is revealed in Christ Jesus our Lord. Romans - 8:37-39

Every person has experienced brokenness, wounded-ness, fear, doubt, and distress. I've been blessed to hear the stories of many of my women friends, but there are countless others left untold. I am telling you my story, not because I want you to feel sorry for me, or because there's something that makes me different from any other woman; I'm telling you this because I want you to see God at work in my life and know that He is also working in your life, as well. I am sharing what I know to be true about God.

Six years ago, I went on an ACTS retreat for the first time. There were women there who listened to me, cried with me, prayed with me as I shared how I feared my marriage was over. I was utterly dependent on my husband for everything; my self-esteem rested in what he thought of me, and how he received the things I did and said and thought. I depended on how he provided for me. All I had ever wanted to be was a wife and mother; I was devastated that our marriage was collapsing and there was nothing I could do to stop it; we tried counseling, but as my counselor said, *"That only works if both sides want it to."*

I had gone back to work teaching in a Catholic school. I had no idea how I would be able to live independently; to support myself and care for our four children. My self-esteem was so low that I believed I was at my husband's mercy; I felt like he took advantage of my low self-esteem in our divorce proceedings. I was at my very lowest. I was lost, afraid, and couldn't see how I was going to survive on my own.

I believe God used my retreat experience to show Himself to me when all else fails. After my first retreat, I spent the next year of my life, during our separation and divorce proceedings, in the adoration chapel at church. I read my Bible and prayed in that small room. I cried out to the Lord and hoped he heard me. I survived and my children are thriving. They are without a doubt the best things to come out of that marriage, and for that alone, I am thankful.

Six years later, I am still teaching in a Catholic school. I don't think I could teach anywhere else. It is my vocation. Catholic schoolteachers still don't earn very much, but you know what? It's enough. God always makes a way, and I am able to provide for my children and myself. I find myself looking ahead to graduating from the University of the Incarnate Word with my M.Ed. I now have the confidence to apply for the PhD program with the dream of becoming a professor. I have discovered that I am satisfied with my life and the direction it is heading. I am now the decision maker, the fixer, and the person in charge. I have a renewed sense of confidence; I'm finding success at work and at grad school.

None of these things would have happened if I had stayed in my marriage. I was a shell of the person I am today, and it is only through the grace of God that I've come this far. I finally feel like things are on track. And I like it this way. Things are looking up and I am looking to the future. God has a funny way of putting things back into focus. And by that, I mean into focus on Him.

One day while I was in the shower I felt something that caught me off guard; a lump on my breast. I called my doctor and we immediately scheduled an appointment with radiologist for a mammogram.

Right around this time, I was invited to serve on an ACTS retreat team. I was hesitant at first...I had so much on my plate. But I felt God telling me to say *"yes."* When I learned that our scripture was Psalm 46:10 *"Be still and Know that I Am God,"* I felt such a sense of peace. I knew that this was meant to be.

The mammogram came, the day after my birthday. I didn't say anything to anyone because I didn't want anyone to freak out. I didn't want to worry anyone unnecessarily. After the mammogram, the radiologist said *"biopsy."* My heart dropped. It was not because I was scared of what it would show, but because I knew in my heart...even before all the tests, that this was going to be what I expected all along.

Two days after my biopsy, I checked my voice mail and without even hearing the results, I knew. I could hear the weariness in my doctor's voice as she urged me to just call her back as soon as possible. It was 9pm. and when you call the doctor at 9pm, you get a recording: *"If this is a medical emergency, please dial 911."* Clearly wanting your biopsy results are not worthy of a call to emergency services. Even if every fiber of your being is screaming out for answers.

The next best option was just to go to bed. How do you sleep knowing you have to make a call in the morning that will change your life? I started wondering if I could get someone to cover my classroom, so I could call first thing, but would I be able to maintain my composure in front of my first graders? Could I keep this deep sadness and fear hidden long enough to get through the day?

I started thinking of all I had planned: I have 4 courses left to take until I graduate; will I be able to finish school? How many sick days do I have left? Can I afford to miss work? Will I still be able to teach? Will I be able to finish out the school year? Will I be able to come back next year? I refused to let myself think about my own sweet precious children. That was too painful: It is much easier to think about the practical things...well, not that that is easy, but so much harder to think how this will affect the ones I love the most in this world.

The next morning at 9:00am while teaching math class, the doctor calls me. The secretary comes to get me, and I just know. I walk past my friend's second grade classroom that I had already talked to about my situation and she followed me to the nurse's office where I could take the call in private. I hear the words "cancer" and "surgeon" and oncologist." I hung up the phone and my friend cried with me.

In the middle of this, God asks me to be still. This is good, because I can't pray. My heart is paralyzed. The words don't come. And then when they do, they sound insincere, banal. How do I ask him to take this from me, when clearly there's a reason for all this? How do I choke out the words, *"Heal me."* In the back of my mind I wonder if by asking for healing, he'll give me instead the ultimate healing my soul yearns for, but my heart and mind and body are not ready for? I have too many things left unfinished: I'm not done being a mama. I'm not ready to stop being a student. I'm not ready to give up that classroom of wonder-filled first graders.

The days that follow are a blur; it moves so quickly that before I know it, I'm meeting with doctors and having tests done, surgery scheduled to place my port for chemotherapy. My dear friend goes with me to every single one of these appointments. She takes notes and asks the questions I can't even think of.

I started asking God to reveal Himself to me. And He did. I saw Him through the people He put in my path. From the oncologist who stated she is a "God girl," to the surgeon whose online profile stated he was an active member in his church, and who also displays a Bible on the table in his waiting room.

I felt God's presence everywhere; significant songs that came on the radio out of nowhere; prayers from people I knew and people I didn't know; with constant phone messages and texts that came at just the moments when I needed them the most.

And then there was my professor who was such an inspiration at this difficult time. She inspired me in so many ways. She was a single mom for a long time and continued to pursue her education while her children were growing up. The thing I admire most is that she is unashamed of her faith. She says at the end of every class, *"I taught in public schools for so many years and was never allowed to pray. I'm at a private school and I can pray… so let's pray."* and she does.

At the start of the semester, I emailed my professor to let her know what was happening with me, and she was always very supportive. So, when she prays for us, at the end of class…for obstacles to be removed from our paths, for wellness and healing, for strength in the face of struggles, I know that while she asks these things for all her students, she is also praying for me, intentionally.

I thank God for never leaving my side, especially during those times when I hated what I was going through: the chemo, the hair loss and feeling horrible. He helped me to go through the motions of my daily life in a purposeful way.

I had my mastectomy in July 2015 and on the 21st, my oldest son's birthday. My surgeon called me and said, *"Not only are you cancer-free, but there was absolutely no evidence of the disease."* He stated that he's only seen this once in his practice with cases like mine. I continue to be cancer-free – three years and counting!

I graduated with my master's degree in education in December of 2015, with a 4.0 grade point average. In my final semester, my dear professor that I referenced earlier was also diagnosed with breast cancer. Awful as that is, I know God brought us together for a specific reason. As she had prayed for me, I began to pray for her: for obstacles to be removed from her path, for wellness and healing, and for strength in the face of struggle. She too is now cancer-free.

I continue to feel God at work in my life, but not always as plainly and as obviously as He did in those dark days. But I know that He is there, that He loves me, and He will never leave me. – *Amy Migura*

Reflection: Faith is trust, assurance and confidence in God. Faith is the belief that an existence is there, even though you don't see or are able to touch it. The virtue of faith allows one to believe that with God anything and everything is possible. – Henry Trevino)

Around the Bend, Blessings Appear

We hope for what we don't have yet. So we are patient as we wait for it. Romans 8:25

It never entered my mind that I would be a widow at the age of 48. How could this happen to me? I was happily married to a man I loved dearly. We often talked and made plans for our retirement. My husband Bert and I had been married for almost eight years. This wasn't supposed to happen to us. Was I forsaken by my God, my God whom I prayed to every day?

The hardest part of Bert's death was the acceptance of the way he died. For the first year following my husband's death, I kept a journal of all the things I was experiencing. From morning to night I continuously made notes of all the little things that brought us together. I missed him terribly. Writing on a daily basis was helpful and therapeutic during my grieving process. I started to slowly learn how to survive the suicide of my husband, one day at a time.

After that difficult first year, as I went back through my journal entries, it was evident that I had written them while in a cushion of shock. I realized how raw and intense my feelings were, as if I hadn't experienced them before. As I continued reading more journal entries, it was clear to me that I did not remember writing them. I felt this strange feeling come over me, which proved to me that God had me in the palm of his hands all along.

I had no choice but to relive the tragedy of the year before. I had no option but to remember my great loss in order to move on in my grieving process. All the while, the reality of my loss began sinking in. I had no idea how I survived that first year; all I remember is that I was in constant prayer.

Reliving my heartbreak is what ultimately saved me. I believe now more than ever that in order to get through something, you have to truly experience it no matter how hard it is. I had to feel and deal with everything that was coming to the surface. Only then, could I get to a place of peace and acceptance.

After more than two years of grieving for the loss of my husband, I felt that I was ready and open to love again. Up until that time I had dated occasionally, but my heart was in a place where I didn't want to just date. I wanted to be in a relationship that was going to have a future. I was 50 at the time, and I wasn't into dating. I just wanted someone to magically pop into my life out of nowhere. I turned it over to God and always believed in my heart that God would work things out if I just remained patient.

Initially I began accepting dates from friends of friends. Eventually I went beyond my comfort zone and did a little experimenting on an online dating site. I was a bit embarrassed and somewhat apprehensive to admit that, but it seemed like it would be easy enough. I was disappointed to say the least because my venture did not go very well. I decided to take a break and reassess my thinking. I deleted my account and my profile on the dating site.

After closing my dating account, I wanted to stay busy and forget my desire to date. I viciously started cleaning and rearranging the house. I got rid of all the things that were keeping me stuck in the past. One morning I sat down to check my emails. I hadn't received any notifications from the dating site since I cancelled it. Then it happened; out of nowhere, someone nudged me and sent me an email. How did someone get through when I was no longer active on that site?

I ended up accepting this person's nudge to communicate by email. At first, I was somewhat hesitant to accept the email, however, I liked his pictures that he had posted on his profile. The one thing that troubled me was that he was working in Afghanistan. I remember thinking to myself; I haven't been able to meet anybody in the city where I live, what are the chances of this going anywhere, especially since he was on the other side of the world. I had already turned this whole issue over to God and had been feeling confident that since God was in control, anything could happen when I least expected it. I proceeded with caution, after all what could he do from Afghanistan?

After a couple of emails back and forth to each other I learned that his name was Ernest, although it didn't dawn on me that he went by Ernie. I remember smiling the moment I realized that. My late husband, Bert was a jokester. I had a feeling that if he had any part of this arrangement, he too would give me a sign. What are the chances of all the names in the world, that my beloved Bert would send me someone named "Ernie" to fill that void in my life. Bert used to tell me that as far back as he could remember, people would always ask him jokingly, *"Hi, Bert, where's Ernie?"* They are the infamous pair from the show *Sesame Street*. This is when I knew for certain that, as far out there as it seemed, anything and everything was possible.

We communicated by email, text, even by phone for almost three months while he was in Afghanistan. I think one of the first things that seemed to connect us was our sense of humor. We had plenty of time to get to know each other. I felt that both of us knew in our hearts that we had met for a reason. How many people nowadays fall in love before they even meet in person. It is an unusual and exciting adventure that is part of our love story.

Upon his return to the states he came straight to San Antonio. We were married two months later. That was over seven years ago, and we are still very happily married. We spend most of our days laughing and relishing the thought of us being married.

I sincerely believe in my heart that God does work things out in his time and in his own way, usually in a way that we would least expect it. There is no way that I could have orchestrated or had anything to do with how I met my husband. He was working on the other side of the world in a remote location, on a not so popular dating site, that I had actually cancelled. All unfolded exactly how God wanted it to. Now our lives are complete, and we are very grateful for God's help in bringing us together. I never could've have imagined the blessings that were waiting for me just around the bend. – *Letty Ramirez*

Reflection: The death of your loved one is one of the hardest heartbreaks to accept. Only time can temper the loss of your soul mate. Once time has lessened the pain of the loss, you must continue to move past the grief and regret. You should not allow the past to dominate the rest of your life because like all other endings, some doors will close and other doors will open to new and exciting beginnings. – Henry Trevino

Blessed With a Baby

They will be like the dust of the earth that can't be counted. They will spread out to the west and to the east. They will spread out to the north and to the south. All nations on earth will be blessed because of you and your children after you. Genesis 28:14

Yep, a baby is on the way. I waited eight days before I took a pregnancy test. It was faint, but it was there. I was in denial, but Jaime, my husband, was sure he could see that line. So, I took another test, and another, and another and another. I took six pregnancy tests over the course of four days. After the third one though, I believed deep down that it was very possible. I was crying, scared, and unprepared. Jaime on the other hand was laughing at me in a completely cool manner. He seemed so relaxed while I felt like I could faint. He was so supportive and said over and over again, *"It is going to be fine, and don't worry, we are ready."* I guess you never really know how you're going to feel in that moment when you realize your life is about to drastically change, and for me it was a little scary.

At 14 1/2 weeks, I finally feel as though I can start embracing this whole pregnancy thing and allow it to settle in. The weeks before, I had been somewhat cautious. I'm fully aware of the things that can happen, and I just want to be realistic. I consider every pregnancy and birth an actual miracle so I'm so thankful for where I am now.

In a conversation with my mom and my aunt, *(who both had no idea what they were having when they were pregnant)* I thought about how exciting it was for them to be completely surprised, I decided that I did not want to find out the gender either. Jaime is a very simple and easygoing man; he was totally fine with it.

The way I see it, is that my life with baby will start when he/she is born. I can prepare everything the same from the room, to the clothes, to the name. I always imagined my baby room pretty simple to begin with, having a modern and bohemian vibe. I seem to have let go of needing all *"the perfect things."* All the material things don't seem to matter either.

What I am most excited about is getting the most perfect baby, boy or girl. Not knowing the gender before it arrives won't let me know who this child is going to be or how a baby will fit in my life. It won't make me more connected to it emotionally. It will not make any difference at all. The baby is still growing in my belly; his or her facial features will still be a mystery to me. I will meet this gorgeous baby when the time comes, just like everyone else. I know my heart and I know that any child I created with my husband will be the one that God created specifically for us.

I feel good about where I am right now and living in this moment. My body is adapting well to baby growing inside me. I am still working out 4-5 times a week. I'm mixing strength training, yoga, and even spin classes sometimes. I modify by moving slower. My doctor told me to do workouts I can endure, not where I'm counting down the seconds till it's over. It's been great to be able to still move my body; it's what I am used to, and I get pretty cranky if I skip out.

I haven't had too many aches/pains (yet). I am so enjoying watching my body transforming. It sounds crazy, but I've never had my body speak so loudly to me than during this pregnancy. It's constantly communicating and telling me what I need more or less of; Charlie horse, drink more water, fatigue, sit down and rest, hungry, eat, heartburn, well, deal with it, can't breathe, change positions. The list goes on.

I look at photos of my ever-changing body and don't see me anymore. I see a baby growing inside me. Not just any baby, but a baby Jamie and I created. It's the most magical thing I have ever experienced in my life. A feeling I can't put into words. A feeling I never want to let go of or forget. Now that it's moving and grooving in there, we have multiple conversations a day.

The moment I wake up and I don't feel my baby, I give it a little shake to wake up, it kicks back, and then my heart is happy. Over the last few weeks, I've learned the times of day now when baby sleeps, and I know the times of day when it's up playing, learning, and growing. Every time I'm walking or working out, I know that these movements are attaching to the baby and will eventually be what puts him/her to sleep when our baby is born. The "sshhing" sound will remind the baby of my blood moving and heart beating. The rocking will feel like my footsteps. The swaddle will feel like its tight, little womb. Everything I do on the outside will be a thing that reminds it of home. My body now feels like it's not my own, baby owns it now!

I am blessed to have had such a smooth pregnancy with no sickness, food aversions, nothing. Since I'm a really active person it's been pretty hard for me to sit still when I am used to going on long walks, working out, and doing yoga multiple times a week. None of that stuff feels good at the moment so I'm going to have to get creative. I will continue to monitor, modify, and take days off by being aware of what my body is trying to tell me.

My due date is approaching rather fast. I'm going to miss everything about being pregnant so I'm enjoying every last little thing about this wonderful experience. My belly is growing along with my baby, who is squirming inside me. My emotions are up and down, feeling the nerves and excitement for what lies ahead. Everyday takes a little more effort to relax and unwind because after all, baby could come any day now. How does one prepare for mommy hood? I really don't know, and I think I won't know until I am actually living it. Up until that point though, there's nine months of thinking, and I've definitely done that. I've thought about who the baby will be, how he or she will fit into our lives, how I will be fully responsible, how we will manage it all…you name it; I've thought about it. Every time I feel a little kick, it's another reminder of this new baby coming into our lives in a very short time. It's so exciting and so scary at the same time.

At last the due date has arrived, but baby is still in my belly. It seems like I got a burst of energy on this particular day. In my conversation with baby I assure my little one that I am feeling positive and not scared at all. I've got your grandmas here, your dad, bubba and you in my belly. Everyone's ready. It's very safe in there I know, but I think you'll like it out here too; no, I'm positive you will. I've prayed everyday about this miracle inside me and have told my baby over and over that we will love him/her no matter its gender, its personality, its likes and dislikes. We are now just patiently waiting for the arrival of our baby into this world and cannot wait to shower it with all of our love.

Two days after my due date, I gave birth to our precious little girl and we named her Poppy Jay Scope. We thank God for blessing us with this beautiful little bundle of joy. It never mattered to us whether the baby would be wrapped in a blue or a pink blanket; the true blessing is what was inside. "A baby." – *Jaimee Hart Scope*

Reflection: It is said that the apple doesn't fall far from the tree. Lay the groundwork so that your children will be a people of faith, so that they will learn from you the meaning of life. The lessons you impart into their being will give their character meaning and they will truly be a seed from where they came. – Henry Trevino

Faith's Story

He said to her, "Daughter, your faith has healed you. Go in peace freed from your suffering." Mark 5:34

My struggles started when I was five or six years old. I lived from day to day not knowing how my days were going to turn out, as my dad's lifestyle was in and out of prison. My mom didn't want me; in fact, I think she hated me. Maybe it was because of the fact that I was born, or maybe just because I was my dad's child. My mom would stuff me with pink square pills, eventually putting me in a mental hospital where I almost died. I was moved to my grandma's house and she became my guardian. She raised me the best she could with what little she had. I know that she was not aware of anything that I had been going through. My grandma taught me most of what I know, and the rest was picked up in the neighborhood or on the streets.

On my dad's side of the family, one by one, my uncles, cousins, and even my grandpa sexually abused me. They would sometimes bribe me with candy, chips and toys. I never spoke about it because I was scared. I was just a little girl and thought I would get in trouble if I said anything. I didn't know if what was happening to me was good or bad. I felt so alone, and I was desperate to talk to someone.

When my dad wasn't in prison, he was very loving and protective of me. If he knew what others were doing to me, he would have put a stop to it. My dad used to write letters to me and send me drawings.

That all changed when my dad met Yvonne. They met when my dad was in prison. They lived together but never got married. She had two daughters, Faran, and Emily. I never would have thought, that one day, my dad would be included with the rest of them that would sexually abuse me.

The sexual abuse by my father was the worst and scariest thing I ever experienced. One day he even tried to kill me; he threw me on the floor and jumped on me and started choking me with both hands. The only thing that saved me was when my uncle walked in the house.

Yvonne also became very mean to me. She would make me kneel down against the wall, sometimes all day and night. I went to school only when Yvonne said I could go, if I annoyed her in any way, she would tell my dad and he would whip me. She would only feed me when she thought I deserved it, and sometimes she would not even let me use the bathroom. She was so angry with me one time that she threw a screwdriver at my head, but fortunately I moved just in time and the screwdriver missed me and stuck in the wall. She was really the personification and embodiment of an evil stepmother.

I found out that what was happening to me was also happening to my older sister Jasmine. I witnessed it with my own eyes and when I mentioned it to my mom in front of my dad, she just turned around and slapped me. One night while sleeping, I heard a noise that woke me up. It was Yvonne's young daughter, Emily, who was also being molested by my dad. The next day I confronted her and although she denied it, she began crying. I said, *"It's ok, you can trust me, because it's happening to me too."* We hugged and cried together, but after that, my dad tried to keep us apart.

Yvonne's two daughters were her pride and joy; I was just the burden. She knew that I had no one to protect me so the punishments got worse. I wonder if she enjoyed calling me bad names; I was 12 years old and stunned at the way she talked to me.

My dad, also ruined the only real relationship I had, with my grandmother. He told her that I was a big liar, and that I was trying to break him up with his girlfriend. My grandmother, with tears in her eyes says, *"Why are you doing this to your dad?"* My heart was broken; I told her, *"I'm not trying to hurt you, I love you too much."* She just continued crying and then informed me, that she was homeless too, so I needed to go back with my dad.

The abuse continued, physical, sexual, and verbal. Not only from my dad, but other people who were associated with family members. I was always staying at other's people homes, with different family members mostly, but always only temporary. It also seemed like I was always the reason we had to leave. It seemed that everywhere I went, people abused me, blamed me for things that were not true, accused me of inappropriate behavior, inappropriate dress, stealing, and causing all the drama that seemed to follow me wherever I went. There seemed to be no one that I could really trust. The few people I thought I could trust ended up hurting me.

By the time I was 15, I started going out with friends, staying out late, sometimes two or three days at a time. I would stay here and there with different guys, drinking and popping pills. I had a couple of boyfriends during this difficult time in my life, but they never worked out and ended up turning into abusive relationships. I was always the one who was to blame for everything that happened to me; it was my fault that I was cheated on, my fault that I was raped, or drugged or beaten up.

After the breakup of a dysfunctional relationship that lasted for 12 long years, I tried to take my own life. Luckily help came quickly and I survived. Deep down, I really didn't want to kill myself. I was just mad at myself for wasting all those years on someone that wasn't good for me. I realized I hadn't done anything for myself to be more independent. I had a couple of odd jobs here and there, but I was finally ready to take responsibility for my own life, by the decisions and choices I made.

Not long after making the decision to get my life together, I was at my job, when I had a complete nervous breakdown. They took me to a counselor who recommended that I should be checked into a mental hospital. My stay at the hospital was only two days and they let me go.

I realized I was working trying to better my situation, and myself, but yet I wasn't being honest with myself. The guy I was living with at the time was just for convenience to both of us. He had a drinking problem and the little money I was making was going towards his liquor. I was overwhelmed and guess it just got to me. It did make me realize that I was being taken advantage of again, so it was time to move on.

The night I left the hospital I received an odd Facebook message. It read; *"Hola Preciosa."* The message was from a guy named Nathan. It turned out that he was a friend of the guy I was staying with. They both played on the same soccer team.

I really didn't care for the guy at first, but after about a week of talking to him, I started to become interested. One weekend Nathan came around and picked me up and we just hung out. I honestly had the best time I had ever had. He took me here and there and unlike other guys he was a gentleman. While we were out, he paid for everything. Nobody had ever done that for me. I remember telling him not to fall for me because I wasn't good for him. I joked with him by telling him that I was going out with him just to make his friend jealous.

It was during this weekend, I realized that I really liked him and that we could make something out of our friendship. I got the courage and asked him if he wanted me to be his girlfriend. *"All you have to do is ask,"* I said. He did ask me, and I said, *"Hell yes."*

Nathan and I have been together since March 5, 2017. We have been inseparable and really enjoy each other's company. He has been so good to me that I love him more every day. He has done his best to build me up and not drop me down. He has put my past behind us and wants only what's best for me; he gives me things I've never had. He fights for me when I can't fight for myself. He's the best man I have ever known.

Every day I wake up and thank God, for placing Nathan in my life. He is a hardworking man who takes nothing for granted, because he came from nothing. It makes me appreciate him that much more. I'm grateful each day we are together and pray that "we" last a lifetime.

I look forward to all life has to offer. I thank God for the many blessings he has given me and wait patiently for all the other blessings I know are on the way. I am so grateful for the amazing job I have at the gym. I have wonderful people I work with who encourage and inspire me. My hope now, is to continue what I'm doing to help myself feel better; exercising, watching what I eat, and perhaps lose a little weight so that one day I can have a child of my own. I trust God; he knows what he's doing, as well as all the hopes and dreams I have in my heart.

Sometimes, I think about how I survived all the events that took place in my life and know that I did not get through it with my own strength. I know God was there with me and I have faith and believe that God will never leave my side.

I hope that my story will help someone who is suffering from things that happened in their past, things that haven't been processed, keeping you from peace and acceptance. While writing my story it caused everything I was feeling to rise to the surface, to face it and then erase all the bad things that happened to me. It has been a tremendous self-therapy.

One day, out of the blue, my father asked me to forgive him; my response to him was, *"I forgive you, but really, God is the one you're going to have to answer to."* I don't have hate in my heart now. It was a hard process to forgive all the people who had hurt me. But, I'm grateful to experience what true love really feels like. – *Faith*

Reflection: You can say to yourself; "I lived through this horror. I know I can take the next thing that comes along." The resiliency of an individual and the belief in God translates to the inner strength that everyone possesses. By all means you can rest assured that encountering another fearful shock will not be something that will conquer or defeat you. – Henry Trevino

From Rags to Riches

So do not fear, for I am with you; do not be dismayed, for I am your God. I will strengthen you and help you; I will uphold you with my righteous right hand. Isaiah 41:10

A baby was born to an immigrant family in the early 1930s. He was the eldest of three brothers. The baby was born in a small house in back of a grocery store that his father had opened with $50.00 borrowed from a friend. Another friend in the grocery business let him have ten pounds of hamburger meat on credit. The baby was born into this poverty-stricken family. The father and mother had a limited education, having only gone to the third grade in school. Their desire was to be sure that their baby would have a high school education

The baby's father worked from 4 a.m. till 10 p.m. seven days a week in that little grocery store. The baby's mother also tended to the few customers that came to buy what few items that were on the shelves. As time passed the baby grew into a toddler that was taught a very frugal lifestyle. Any luxury extras never came about. For a play pistol he played with the jawbone of an ox. For transportation he rode a broomstick and pretended it was a horse. He was taught that life depended on work. Food was not to be wasted and the baby's mother cooked only enough to satisfy the stomach for that one meal. During the winter months two rooms of their little home were closed for the duration of the winter. This was done to conserve fuel that was used in the wood-burning stove.

The baby was the second to be born to this impoverished family. The first-born died as an infant due to sickness and the hardships of the Great Depression. All through these hardships this small family survived with a lot of love and care. The baby did not learn to speak English until he was about eight years old. When he turned seven he was sent to a school where the only language spoken was English and if you spoke any other language you were ordered to stand in the corner.

When the little boy was in the third grade he was enrolled in a Catholic school. The school was so small that they had one room with pupils from the fourth, fifth and sixth grade. All were taught by one nun. As the years passed, this little boy was enrolled into a school for boys. Again, as in the past, the male teachers never hesitated to inflict physical punishment. This young fellow never did partake in school activities. He had to go straight home to help in the small grocery store his father owned.

During the last two years of high school this young man held down three jobs. After the lunch hour he helped clean and mop the cafeteria. After school he helped in the grocery store. After the store closed at 6 p.m. he went to work for a company that was taking a census for a phone directory. All three jobs paid him less than twenty dollars a week. He remembered an event that helped him succeed and gave him the determination to forge ahead. During a history class in the tenth grade in high school, the professor decided to digress and predict who was going to college and who was not. Well, you guessed it. The professor looked at the young boy and told him to his face that he would never attend college. He added that the boy would never see the inside of a college. This one incident made up the young boy's mind.

The boy graduated from high school in three and a half years. He enrolled in a university. While going to college he continued working. He worked at a meat packing plant all night. In the morning he would shower at work and go straight to the university.

During his first year in college this young man married his teenage sweetheart. A year and a half later they had a son. Two years later another baby came into their life. All the time the young man continued working and going to school. After four years of schooling he graduated with a degree in business administration and a minor in finance.

After college he went to work for a finance company. Later he took the test and became a real estate broker. Five years after graduating from school three more children came along making it a total of five babies coming into the boy's marriage. Eventually the real estate market stagnated and the need for more income became critical. He decided to apply for acceptance to the city fire department. He advanced through the ranks to attain the position of captain. In the tests for these positions, he always came in first or second.

After 35 years in the fire service he retired. By no means did he retire to a rocking chair. He has since been elected to 6 different boards of directors. He personally directs investments for two charitable organizations in the fire department. He is a trustee in one health organization that has investments in excess of $360,000,000.00. His hobbies are hunting, fishing, running and weightlifting. His wife of 30 years was suddenly taken from him by a previously undiagnosed illness. He was left with a nine-year-old child still at home. In spite of his misery, he willed himself to live and continue raising his son.

His young son is now in the fire service as are his other two brothers. The oldest child has now retired from the fire service. The number three son was a captain in the fire service, having taken the position created when his father retired at the same station with the same crew. He was promoted to the rank of District Chief and is now the Emergency Manager for San Antonio. His number five son also works at the fire station where his father worked. He has been promoted to the rank of captain. He is now on the list to be promoted to district chief. His daughter is working for a university in the recruitment department. She graduated from Incarnate Word University with a degree in organizational psychology and has attained a master's degree from Texas University. His 2nd son is a graduate of West Point and has now retired from the U.S. Army.

This is that young boy's life. It was shaped, by perhaps a well-intentioned yet callous professor who predicted that this young man was not college material. – *Henry Trevino*

Reflections: From the moment of birth your life will face constant challenges. A challenge is not a dare; it is a test of your willingness to respond. Responding to a challenge is not about education or a desire; the response is determined by one's fortitude and courage to follow through. – Henry Trevino

God Was Truly My Savior

God is our place of safety. He gives us strength. He is always there to help us in times of trouble. Psalm 46: 1

My story started on a warm August night. Our crew had just returned from fighting a three-hour fire. I cleaned up and jumped into the sack. As I lay there I started laughing. I was laughing about the restaurant patrons streaming out of the restaurant that was on fire. The fire department had responded to a fire at the same restaurant a few weeks before. As we entered the restaurant, we saw plates with half-eaten food. It was a grease fire that we quickly extinguished.

I was in bed and almost asleep when I heard an all-familiar beep. Whenever a fire was reported the fire alarm dispatch office alerted us with three "beeps." The speaker in the dormitory issued the words; *"Regular Alarm, Regular Alarm, Center and North Olive."* Over the speaker, the dreaded words that we never wanted to hear came over the loudspeaker; *"Possible victim trapped in the structure."*

We slid the pole and mounted the pumper and left the fire station with emergency lights on and siren wailing to alert traffic. Even though the fire was about two and half miles from the station we could see the glow of the fire in the night sky. We knew we had a working fire.

Engine Company #3 was the first arriving company at the scene. They reported a "working fire on a two-story house." They asked the second company to lay a supply line to the fireplug. Engine Company #1 arrived and laid a supply line to Engine Company #3. Engine Company #3's crew was attacking the fire on the front porch. While #3 was fighting the fire on the porch, other firefighters were taking an injured firefighter off the porch.

Engine Company #3 was a block from the fire, so they did not have time to don their breathing apparatus. I was acting officer on Engine Company #7. We were the last company to arrive at the scene. By the time we got to the fire my crew and I had had time to don our masks and proceeded to enter the structure and commence rescue operations. As we entered, we could see heavy smoke and fire at the top of the stairwell.

I took #3's nozzle and proceeded up the stairs. As soon as I opened the nozzle, I dropped through the floor of the first stair landing. As I fell, I managed to suspend myself on the floor joists. Another firefighter was trying to help keep me from falling all the way through the floor. As I hung there, I could feel that I was burning from the fire below.

I managed to put my hands on the floor and tried to push myself up. As I tried to push myself up my hands went through the charred floor. As my hands fell through the floor my bunker coat was pushed up exposing my arms and my wrists. Burning embers fell into my exposed gloves and my wrists and hands became unbearably painful. For a moment I thought that I should just let myself fall through the floor and try to get out from the burning bottom floor. Eighteen years of firefighting experience told me to just hang there and let other firefighters get me out.

As the rescue proceeded, the firefighters had to leave me and pick up the nozzle to spray the fire so it would not completely overtake us. As I hung there, I felt that I was really jammed into a hole and had the feeling that I was not going to get out alive. I began to pray the Lord's Prayer. I had reached the second verse when I felt myself being bounced down the stairs. Firefighters had taken me out of the hole and were trying to take me out of the building. The last thing I remember was my air tank bouncing on each step and hurting my back. I finally felt myself being carried out to the front lawn.

I was immediately taken to the burn ward at Fort Sam Houston. I was in the hospital for one month. The surgical procedures were extremely painful. I received a large skin graft to my right thigh. I had 3rd degree burns to my hands and wrists. After a month in the hospital, undergoing surgical procedure after surgical procedure and enduring unrelenting pain I was released but continued to receive medical care. I eventually returned to full duty months after the fire. I must say that the long stay at the hospital was the most painful experience of my life.

As a recap, the fire investigators found that gang members had doused the building with gasoline hoping to burn another gang member who had invaded their neighborhood. The gang member that was trapped in the house saved himself by sliding down a drainpipe from the second floor.

I will always remember what the nuns at Saint John Berchmans Catholic School taught us. They told us that we should never ask God for selfish want or reasons; that we should always pray for those that are in true need. When a time comes that you are in true need of him, He will be there for you. All you need to do is ask. – Hector Cardenas

Reflections: It is said that when all else fails one should turn to prayer.... for God in his mercy will never turn you away. Prayer is a very special way of talking to God our creator. God hears our prayers and will always answer them. – Henry Trevino

God is Good

My God will meet all your needs. He will meet them in keeping with his wonderful riches. These riches come to you because you belong to Christ Jesus. – Philippians 4:19

By the grace of God, our house sold in 11 days. It was a smooth transaction and we sold it for the asking price. Immediately we found a townhome to rent and knew it was the one, before we actually even saw it. I of course had been praying for a sign, and when I found out the street name was the name of my grandson, I knew without a doubt that this was the one we were supposed to rent.

The ironic thing was the timing. The day we moved was the same day it was announced that we would not be going back to school from our spring break. I work as an assistant teacher and was grateful our spring break had been during that week. I thought another week at home would be great. I could get a lot more unpacking done. I had no idea we were going to experience an unprecedented pandemic. As of now it has been one month being stuck at home and it's looking like we are going to be quarantined for at least another few weeks.

During this time, I reflected on the how things had unfolded in the last month. I hadn't wanted to move; I loved my house. We enjoyed living there, especially the use we were getting with the pool in the backyard. I used it on daily basis for exercise plus it was so fun and convenient having a pool in the backyard when the grandkids came to visit. We loved being outside, barbequing, working on the yard and then jumping in the pool. We have such hot weather all year round, we couldn't even imagine not having a pool, and it would be boring.

Although my husband makes good money, I recently went back to work so maybe we could pay off some old debts, it just seemed that the more money we made it was never quite enough, and my bills never seemed to change.

I am somewhat of a private person, and so most people didn't really know how much I have always struggled with my finances. As long as I can remember I've lived paycheck to paycheck; when unexpected things came up, I depended on God. He always provided what we needed when we needed it. I cannot even remember when I didn't pray to God to help me with my finances. Yes, he always came through but I looked forward to the day I would get a big break and we could just start over. My husband and I talked a lot about our situation and I always told him to continue praying. I had faith that one-day it would get better. God would show us a way.

One particular evening in his frustration, he glanced at me and said, "I understand that we need to pray but do you think that the money we need is just going to fall from the sky, I feel like we need to do something." My husband has come a long way with his faith, so I was a little disappointed that he was forgetting how big God is and having to remind him of the many miracles we have and continue to witness in our lives. I told him like so many other times before that I didn't know how God was going to get us out of this; I just truly believed he would. Things would change in God's time probably in a way we never could've imagined.

That same evening I received a call from my daughter Emily and my son-in-law; Houston. They knew that we were struggling and wanted to help us. They advised us to sell our house, use the money we make to pay off all our bills, and downsize. I was somewhat shocked, a little angry and very sad. My first thought was, *'No, I don't want to move or sell my house; I loved my house and I loved my pool.'* They were genuine and sincere about helping us and supporting us and offered to take care of the details, we just needed to trust them.

I was embarrassed by what people would think of me, or how they would judge me. I felt guilty for selling this house that I purchased from a family member, within three years, and making a big enough profit to pay off my debts. I felt sad that I wouldn't have the convenience of my backyard pool where I exercised, and I enjoyed swimming with my grandkids.

I didn't really want to go where God was leading me, but I did it anyway. I trusted him and his plan. I knew in my heart that this was probably the answer to my many years of prayer. I decided, like so many other times in my life that I was going to turn it over to God. We decided to put it on the market and see what happens. We were going to "bless it or block it." If it was Gods will for us to sell it and move on, then I just knew it would happen quickly, and if it was not in God's plan for us to move, then it would just not sell or there would be too many obstacles in the way.

It took me a day or two before I really started to think about it. We bought our house at a good price; when we put the numbers together – if we sold it for what we were asking – we would make enough to cover our debt and have a little left over. I knew in my heart that it was the right thing to do. I couldn't help but realize how long I had been praying for our financial situation to improve. Maybe our house was just too much for us. I really only used three rooms in that house anyway. Less house would mean less furniture, less clutter, less maintenance, and since we decided to rent instead of buy, we would not have to worry about unexpected expenses.

This seemed like a very big decision for me and more emotional than I thought it would be. Once I accepted that the only decision I really had to make was, am I going to turn it over to God? Of course, I am; I have to no matter how uncomfortable it might be.

Once I changed my attitude and the negative vibes I had going on, I started to see things in a new light. I told my husband how proud I was of all the work we had both done to update the house. We bought it at a fair price, but we flipped it. We put in a lot of hard work and a little bit of money too. That was the reason we were able to make money plus of course the great housing market had a lot to do with it too. Maybe it was God's plan all along.

My husband and I are not extravagant people. We don't spend money on luxuries or go on trips. We like the simple things in life and have gotten more into "less is more" mentality. I realized how much money we were wasting on trying to get rid of old debt, high interest credit cards with big monthly payments. I wanted to start over. I wanted to use our income for what we needed now, and save the rest. Maybe now we can go on little trips every now and then.

After we closed on the house and received our money, I reminded my husband of the question he asked me a few weeks earlier. "Do you think that by praying, money is going to just fall out of the sky?" We laughed, because that is kind of what happened.

So here we are still in quarantine, but I am so grateful that God allowed things to unfold smoothly and quickly. I can imagine how much worse off we would be had we not made this change literally right before the pandemic when things changed so drastically. God was watching over us. Things are unsettling and times will get harder until we make it to the other side of this pandemic, but I thank God for saving us at a time when things could be so much worse. We are in a better position because of Gods' guidance and having the right people in place to make it all happen. – *Letty Ramirez*

Reflection: Be willing to alter the life you planned and redefine your goals and aspirations. – *Henry Trevino*

Hell on Earth

I can do all this by the power of Christ. He gives me strength- Philippians 4:13.

How well I remember the date, June 5, 1982. I arrived at the training center to get my physical. The results of the physical were ACDURA, (Active Duty for Training). On Monday, June 7, 1982, I arrived at NAV-SEC GRU ACT (Naval Group Security Activity), and checked in. I was immediately assigned to a watch section.

Back in 1982, when we went on our yearly two-week reserve training, we received all the necessary shots so that we would be protected from diseases that were prevalent throughout the world. The following year the injection policy was changed. Apparently, I was not the only one that came down with active transverse myelitis.

On June 10, 1982 I reported to sickbay to get all my required shots. The shots were for malaria, yellow fever, typhoid, tetanus, diphtheria, and smallpox. I was told that I would get a low-grade fever because of the shots. On Wednesday June 16 I started with back pain and my feet felt numb. I thought that I might have overdone my daily workout. On June 17 I reported to sickbay for my final shot—smallpox. I told the corpsman that administrated the shots of my back pain and the numbness I felt. He told me to tell the doctor the next day when I checked out. That next day, I reported to sickbay, however, the doctor was off base. I got no physical examination for release from ACDUTRA. The corpsman gave me my medical records and told me to see my doctor when I got home.

On June 20 I arrived home and could not walk. I had a terrible back pain and my legs and feet felt numb. I called my doctor and he admitted me to the hospital on Monday morning. I was subjected to countless tests from blood samples to myelograms. The next day, Wednesday, the doctor came in and told me I had been diagnosed with transverse myelitis. I had to stay in the hospital 12 days while they loaded me up with antibiotics and steroids.

As days passed, I had to learn to walk and control my pain. I had to concentrate very hard just to walk and do pain management. To make matters worse, I was placed on indefinite sick leave with the fire department and also temporary NPQ (non-drill; non-paid status) with the Reserves by reason of active transverse myelitis.

In December 1982, I was able to go back to drill status with the reserves. In 1983 I was well enough to go back to work in the Fire Department. The final reports given to me by the doctors stated that all the shots that I had taken in 1982 had affected my immune system. The reports stated that I had gotten the virus because of the abnormal immune reactions. Even though I went back to work, my every move had to be carefully calculated and the pain was constant and increasing. While working at the fire department I was assigned to drive one of the district chiefs. I guess you could call it light duty because it had come to the point that it was impossible for me to run, to carry hose, climb a latter or carry an air tank on my back. I finally retired from the fire department in 2005.

My body continued to deteriorate at a faster and faster pace. My back could not hold up my upper body. My upper body started to bend forward at an angle that I could not sustain without holding onto something. I went from cane to walker. Now my immune system is completely messed up. I keep getting coughs and UTIs (urinary tract infections). If I spike a fever it means a week in the hospital. I have gone through all the antibiotics. After the hospital stays comes the rehab, weeks and weeks of rehab. As I get older, I'm having more trouble with bladder and bowel control and walking has become excruciatingly painful and difficult.

My doctor said that as long as I stay active and do some exercise, I might be able to stay out of a wheelchair. Almighty God has given me the determination and will power to keep fighting and exercising. My doctor also told me to file for disability payments back in 1982. Above all my pain and infirmities, I was denied disability assistance, as it was not job related—like being shot or sprayed with Agent Orange. I re-filed for benefits in 2010 and again I was denied. I appealed for a hearing before a judge. The judge was reading through all my reports when he came across a 1982 report from the navy that stated that I was put on non-drill, non-pay status by reason of active transverse myelitis. This report was proof that I was on active duty when I got the virus. Eventually, I got a disability benefit and over the years I'm now getting 90% disability.

    I have now served my hell on earth for over 40 years. I have determined that I am going to stay out of a wheelchair. I try to stay active as much as I can; however, day after day it gets harder and harder. Every morning is a chore just to get up and get ready for the day. My upper body is now bent over to a 90-degree angle. It has become impossible to move without my walker.

    I know that God has been by my side every day of my life. I have felt his presence in my everyday life, and I know full well that he will not abandon me now that I need him the most. I'm sure that God wouldn't send these tribulations my way without extending his helping hand. I firmly believe that with his helping hand I can live the rest of my life in his grace. – *Ed Willborn*

Reflections: God in his infinite wisdom gives us the lesson of serenity, acceptance, courage and wisdom. He gives us the motivation and courage to accept our afflictions. During time of great suffering, one should never forsake God. We should pray to him for he will always be by our side. Like the adage of the two footsteps in the sand; "for that was the time that God carried you."
– *Henry Trevino*

It Goes On

I pray that he will use his glorious riches to make you strong. May his Holy Spirit give you his power deep down inside you. Then Christ will live in your hearts because you believe in him. And I pray that your love will have deep roots. I pray that it will have a strong foundation. Ephesians 3:19

Sixteen; The year I finally got my license and my first car; the year I fell in love with my first boyfriend; the year I became a Junior Varsity cheerleader; the year I lost one of my best friends; the year I truly felt pain; confusion and grief. Your sophomore year in high school is one of transition, development, immaturity, and growth. It's also one of excitement, house parties (sorry Mom) and ever-growing friendships. Not often are people of that age associated with the word *death*. That sentence sounds harsh, doesn't it? Let me be the first to tell you – it was.

Spring break in the year 2010, I was driving home from Destin, Florida, with my then-boyfriend and two of our best friends. We had just spent the best week together and created memories I still hold very close to my heart to this day. We were experiencing our young, wild, and free days.

Upon our return to Texas, spring break wasn't over just yet. It was the last Saturday before school started again. All of us gathered around our friend's house to make sure that this Saturday was a good one, as it always was. Little did I know it was also going to be the last time I would ever see one of my best friends again.

The next morning was something I will never forget. My friend was gone. There had been a car accident after the party and my friend never made it home. We *always* made it home; how could she not be coming home? I had just seen her at the party last night. I had just talked to her; I had just hugged her and told her we'd hang out soon. What do you mean she's *gone?* I had never experienced a phone call like that before; let alone a feeling like that before. The next few days were a complete blur.

Sixteen. That's the age I was when I found power in community, in prayer and in faith. After my friend was gone, all of us stuck together and made sure to honor our friend's memory the best way we knew how. But then again, we were just kids. We all wore blue bracelets with her favorite quote, *Carpe Diem,* for as long as I can remember. My blue bracelet still remains attached to my car keys to this day. If anything came out of this, it's that I learned my friends and I had now shared a bond that couldn't be broken, even if that bond was initially bound by grief.

Nineteen; the age I became a freshman in college; the year my friends started moving all around the world; the year I learned the beginning stages of adulthood; the year it happened again; the year the pain was back.

The heart wrenching pain when you experience the loss of a loved one is stifling. Let's just say it wasn't any easier the second time around. This time though, it was someone who wanted to leave. Another friend of mine had taken his own life at nineteen. It felt like just yesterday the two of us were mourning our friend who had recently died in the car accident and now I mourn them both. I had lost two close friends, but it was different this time. The pain hit differently; the confusion hit harder; the guilt dug deeper.

It's never easy losing someone, be it a grandparent, parent, partner, or in my case, a friend. Death is inevitable, and this story isn't necessarily about my experience or that my pain is any different or greater than yours is or will be. My experience just seemed to happen before I was ready or old enough to handle. But then again, who is ever "ready" for death?

What I will say is that experiencing death at any age is that it never gets any easier. What we have to remember is that the pain stems from love; from the memories shared; from the friendships, relationships, and moments that you created and nurtured and spent with the one you've lost and now mourn.

I am now twenty-six years of age and death continues to go on. But guess what? So does *life*. And so do the memories of the ones you've lost, their stories, their lessons, and their love. It all goes on and you begin to realize how lucky you are to experience these emotions. You begin to become grateful of every moment that passes, because eventually you too, will go on. And that's ok, because with death there was once love and will only continue to be.

Love is at the center of it all, and love is what heals our hearts back together. Eventually we get to a place of peace and acceptance and allow ourselves to open back up to love with the courage and strength to continue on. No one can ask you to forget, no one can tell you how to grieve or how to love or how to feel, and no one can replace the ones we've lost. But we can go on. We can allow ourselves to progress. We can leave it up to God and we can have faith in what will be. And in what will come, because it all goes on. – *Regan Perez*

Reflection: Life should be lived day to day. One can never predict the end. It is said, today is a gift, and tomorrow is a promise." Love and appreciate your friends and the people who have played a part in your life. Remember the many friends that have crossed your path of life and will forever leave footprints in your heart. – Henry Trevino

It Is What It Is

Here is what I am commanding you to do. Be strong and brave. Do not be afraid. Do not lose hope. I am the Lord your God. I will be with you everywhere you go. Joshua 1:9

When I was a little boy, I always wanted to be a fireman, like my dad and my grandfather. I remember going to the station where my dad worked and sitting in the driver's seat amazed at the gadgets, ladders, horns, lights and of course I would love to watch my dad go down the pole.

My mom and dad divorced when I was six years old. Even now as a grown man, I realize how much childhood memories and experiences still weigh heavy on my heart. As a child, some things are so beyond the ability to process in a young mind, that we are left with so many unanswered questions. Over the years, I began questioning what I really wanted to do with my life.

Although my dad was always in my life, my mom remarried when I was still a little boy. My stepdad, Bert was an engineer by trade. I spent a lot of time with him while growing up and I became very interested in the kind of work he did. In fact, I worked with him whenever I could, plus he did many things in and around the house and he made sure I watched him and learned everything that could possibly fit in my head. He would literally take things apart and then tell me to put them back together, but I loved it, and I would not stop until I would figure it out.

Whenever I would mention that I was going to be a fireman, he would tell me, *"No, you are not going to be a fireman, you are going to go to college and get your degree in engineering."* He must have seen something in me that I didn't see. But as time passed, I realized that I really did love building things, and trying to figure out how things worked. I would go to job sites with him, and dream of the day I could drive those forklifts, backhoes, really anything that was big and could be driven.

I had made up my mind when I was still in school that I was going to attend Texas A&M and graduate with a degree in petroleum engineering. Texas A&M had always been the college of my choice, my dream college. My mom was not too keen on the idea of going away for my first two years. She thought it would be better to get my basics out of the way here at home. So, when I received a couple of scholarships at the University of the Incarnate Word my mom decided to enroll me there. I didn't really want to go there, but I made the best of it and even played on the football team that first year.

After attending two years at Incarnate Word I was absolutely thrilled when I was accepted into Texas A&M. I was finally on my way to living the dream. I was so excited, until the unthinkable happened; my stepdad took his life. My life went spiraling down after that. I'm not even sure to this day if I have ever really come to terms with his death. My life was just one big blur for so many years, I'm realizing now that the picture of my life is finally becoming clearer and more focused.

I went through so many emotions during that difficult time in my life. I was angry, grief-stricken, scared, depressed and every other emotion rolled together inside of me with no ounce of relief. I knew that Bert wanted me to go to Texas A&M, because that is where I wanted to go. I had his approval and now because he was no longer here, I knew that I could not leave my mom and my sister alone. It would be too difficult, knowing how hard his death had been on all of us.

I told my friends that I was not going to go to Texas A&M after all, I was going to attend Texas State in San Marcos. I told everyone that one of my best friends decided to go to Texas State and was looking for a roommate. We told everyone that we wanted to go to college and live it up, have some fun. But actually, the real reason was that I could not bear to leave my mom and sister by themselves. They needed me. I think I needed them too. Even though I wanted to leave town my heart wasn't ready; so, I compromised by going away but not too far away.

I spent two years in San Marcos mostly partying and wasting time and money unnecessarily. Things got even worse when I realized that staying at this college was going to push back my graduation timeline. And I was ready to be done. This is when I decided to move back in with my mom; I was tired of this place and so ready to be done with school. I commuted back and forth for a few months, until by the grace of God I managed to return to Incarnate Word where I would be able to graduate a lot sooner.

I felt like I had taken two steps back. I was at the point that I just wanted to graduate. I was working and going to school and so many times I just wanted to give up. I took the fire fighter exam several times with no luck, almost quitting school altogether so that I could go to work full time to make more money. Every day I struggled, it seemed like there was always a million other problems on top of all the other day to day living with school and work. In the back of my mind I knew that I could not give up. I had put in too much time and money to let it all go to waste. There was always that small voice in my head that insisted I could not give up. I know that it was God who gave me the courage, the strength and the will to continue moving toward the goal.

About a year before I was to graduate my girlfriend Ansilee found out we were going to have a baby. We got married and were blessed with a little baby girl. We named her Maci. We continued to live with my mom while we worked, went to school and cared for our baby. I graduated with a degree in engineering and a year later my wife, also graduated.

It has taken me awhile to let go of all the things that I felt were setbacks because they didn't line up with my plans. I realize now that sometimes when we fight so hard to make things go a certain way, maybe it's just not meant to be. I am learning that sometimes all I have to do is to wait and be still and allow God's will to unfold. God's way is always better than mine and comes with less effort on my part.

So, I didn't graduate from my dream college, but I graduated. It took me a little longer than I had planned, but I graduated with an engineering degree. I have a beautiful wife, and two healthy, beautiful children, Maci and Trent. My wife and I bought my childhood home. We both have great and promising careers and are looking forward for many good things to come.

I can't even imagine how we would've made it without the love and support of our families, but God had that figured out, just like everything else. So, now when I have doubts, I remind myself *"Everything is exactly the way it is supposed to be." -- Chris Trevino*

Reflection: Doubts and discouragement can easily sidetrack an idea or a vision. I had my doubts in my younger years, however I regret nothing in my life, even if my past was full of hurt, because it made me who I am today. In retrospect I now know that God walked with me every step of the way and my loved ones encouraged and heartened my resolve to achieve my goal. – Henry Trevino

Las Vegas Massacre

He will cover you with his wings. Under the feathers of his wings you will find safety. – Psalm 91:4

"*Congratulations Michele, you have just won two free tickets to attend the sold-out Route 91 Harvest Festival.*" I stared at this email on my computer and thought, "*No way, did I just win?*" Three days earlier I had submitted my info to a radio subscription service for a chance to win, but wasn't expecting to, as they were only giving away 10 pairs and there were thousands of submissions.

I immediately sent a text to my husband, Will, who of course had no idea, what I was even talking about; he always just goes along. He knows I love all things country and would absolutely not miss 3 awesome days packed with all the artists I love. The next few days we spent figuring out time off from work, hotel accommodations and the dreaded, "*What am I going to wear?*" My husband and I set out to Boot Barn and walked out knowing that we were going to be the best-dressed city country folks in Las Vegas

We woke up Friday morning, dropped the kids off at school, kissed them goodbye and hit the road for the four-hour drive to Sin City. We arrived at our resort, wearing our country gear, unloaded the car, downloaded the Route 91 app on my phone and headed to the venue. I was ready to get started and had our days all planned out.

We arrived a little early before the first act so we managed to sit front row, smack in the middle of the stage. We were having a great time: even my non country-loving husband. He was swaying to the music, fist bumping, and cheering with the strongest swig of whiskey I ever smelt. God bless Will for being dragged into this crazy crowd of 20 something's; he loves to see me happy. We felt like kids again and the best part was that we had two more days of this.

The next day we walked the venue; found the perfect spot to park my cowboy boot wearing feet for the night and enjoy the show. We were much further from the stage, but it gave us a chance to enjoy the show without rowdiness. Surveying the strip around us I mentioned to Will how lucky the people were who were able to stay at the Mandalay Bay and Luxor Hotels. They had prime viewing of the entire venue. It never crossed my mind that evil could be lurking in the city that never sleeps.

Sunday, the last day of our trip, we again, made our way to the festival and planted ourselves in the same seats as the day before. We enjoyed the all-day event but after two full days of heat, walking, dancing and singing I was feeling a bit done.

It was 9:30 pm when I looked at my husband and said, *"Let's go."* Besides, I secretly wanted to hit the roulette table. We started to make our way to the only exit we knew we were allowed to use. I stopped at the midpoint to take a few last pictures since we were now closer to the stage.

My favorite song was just about finishing up; *pop, pop, pop, pop, pop,* the guy in front of us said *"Oh fireworks!"* We all looked up but didn't see anything. Seconds later another round of pops; I looked up and over to my right, to where I hear the sounds and flashes coming from. There in the upper window at the Mandalay Bay something catches my eye. I look to my husband and we both instinctively say *"Gunshots!"* I hear him say, *"Run,"* but my body freezes and I am unable to move.

He drags me to a beer booth; the closest shelter he can find. He ushers me in along with others scrambling for cover. He shouts, *"Get down and cover your head!"* Just then a girl who's been shot is brought in for some kind of medical attention. My husband goes into rescue mode, looks for anything to help stop the bleeding. I see him find a pack of blue rags and he starts applying them to her wounds; one to her chest, the other to her leg.

I can hear people running and screaming in between the brief moments of silence. Bullets begin raining down; this time they're hitting the trailer we are hiding in. I've never been so afraid in my entire life. At that moment all I could think about was my kids. My two youngest were home alone, safe in their beds with no clue mommy and daddy are fighting to stay alive. *Ping, ping, ping, ping*; the bullets sound louder and closer.

Will knows we're not safe but it's not safe out in the open either. I pick my head up and see people running, some are wounded and others helping friends, family or complete strangers. Will shouts, *"We have a girl who has been shot!"* With the help of others, they take her, while all I can hear are her cries of pain. They tell her *"It's going to be ok,"* and that's the last I saw of her.

People everywhere are screaming that a shooter is coming and we need to run but there's no time. My husband ushers us into the freezer the size of a small pantry. It's filled with kegs of beer and it's cold. I'm face to face with a girl who's rocking side-to-side but not fully aware. She whispers, *"I feel light-headed, I think I'm going to pass out."* I grab her arms to steady her and try to keep her awake. I say *"Honey, you need to stay with me because if we have to run, I can't carry you."* All of a sudden it gets quiet; I don't hear gunfire. Will opens the freezer just enough for him to peek out; through the crack I see heavily armed police officers running into the chaos.

Someone yells, *"Get out of there!"* Will throws me over the counter and tells me to run. While running, he notices the girl I was holding was not with us. We promised her we wouldn't leave her but in the chaos, we weren't sure how we had split up. For my husband, no one gets left behind and he was determined to get her out safely.

He tells me to go find somewhere to hide and he'll find me later. Again, I freeze, I was scared and mad that he left me but I also know he wouldn't have left me if he knew I wasn't safe.

I walk around in a circle not sure of where to go or what to do. People are running everywhere, screaming, crying, and bleeding. The police begin to arrive and want everyone to vacate the area. As I walk away from the concert site, I turn around and catch sight of my husband. I have never been more excited to see that man than I was at that moment. He was safe and we were together.

Suddenly, Will breaks down in tears. It's at that moment I notice the blood on his clothes and it's not his. He tells me that after he went back to get that girl there were multiple victims that he assisted to safety and helped load others into vehicles. We sit for a moment trying to soak in what just happened while we console each other. We have held up thus far but at this point we can't take it anymore. We are overwhelmed, emotional, exhausted yet so grateful to be alive.

I don't even remember the walk back to our hotel. I'm tired, hungry and dirty; all I want is to get in our room, lock the door and feel safe. I fall into the bed at 4:15 in the morning but am unable to sleep. I can't get the images of the war zone we escaped out of my head. We turn the news on and just sit in silence as it's being reported the lone gunman has been killed by a self-inflicted gunshot wound.

In hindsight, it was amazing to see people come together in time of need. Seeing so many people putting aside their own injuries to come to the aid of complete strangers who were severely injured was so awe-inspiring.

As a survivor of the worst mass shooting in modern day history, I admit it has changed my life. I now have an additional 21,942 family members and 58 angels looking out for me. Social media has played a huge role in my mental recovery.

Several of my newfound family have started survivor support pages and reading other people's stories and how they were dealing with things has helped me to see that I'm not alone. If I'm having an off day full of anxiety or survivors' guilt, I can turn to anyone of these groups for help or just to vent.

I've tried talking to people who were not at the concert and while I know they are trying to help they just don't understand what I'm dealing with. Having people who have been through the exact same thing as you and can understand the pain and frustration is comforting. Dealing with the trauma isn't always easy. I still look for emergency exits and places to hide when I'm in large crowds. According to my therapist this is my new normal.

As time passes, I'll learn to live with some of these symptoms while others will fade. I will continue to throw on my boots and make that climb. He will not win; I refuse to let him break me. – *Michele Martinez*

Reflection: Fear is a response to a threat of harm. Courage on the other hand is something you must think about. Courage is created at the moment of danger or peril; it is then that you must decide to accept the possibility of harm to yourself or to others. Bravery is what spurs one into action to protect and save fellow human beings out of love, respect and compassion. – Henry Trevino

Lest We Forget

Greater love has no man than to lay down his life for his friends. John 15:13

It was September 11th, 2006, the 5th Anniversary of the 911 terrorists attack on the twin towers. I moved from firefighter to firefighter exchanging greetings and embraces with seasoned veterans and young eager recruits. It was 7am on a muggy Monday morning where a small but proud band of fire fighters was gathering in downtown San Antonio to honor the heroes of 9/11; we planned to march through the heart of the city from Milam Park to the Alamo where we would witness a solemn ceremony remembering those first responders who had made the ultimate sacrifice on that fateful day on September 11, 2001.

Our brothers from the SAPD led the way, clearing the streets and halting traffic for our memorial. As we passed the intersections, the police officers saluted the flags and stood silently at attention. First Units in the parade were Local 624's honor guard and the pipe and drum brigade dressed in their splendid uniforms. Next in line were our antique Coast fire truck and another vintage pumper with veteran fire fighters proudly riding the tailboard of the pumpers. Finally, a contingent of over 100 fire fighters in dress uniforms followed the Fire Department entourage. San Antonio fire fighters and first responders marching in the parade were augmented by first responders from other surrounding towns and cities.

The solemn procession slowly marched down Houston Street. The drums of the fire brigade beat out a slow and deliberated cadence. As we passed, citizens began filling the sidewalks. The canyon formed by the buildings of downtown San Antonio was filled with the magnificent sound of the bagpipes. As the memorial dirge proceeded, the somber music of the bagpipes reverberated against the tall buildings.

As the parade passed, business owners, patrons, workers and visitors were drawn outside. It was all too obvious what this procession was all about. The citizens stood in reverent silence; some removed their hats; others saluted or held their hands over their heart. Some cheered or cried out sincere thanks to all the fire fighters and all the first responders.

For those of us who marched in the parade, our hearts filled with pride; at the same time our hearts felt the sorrow of the great loss. The deliberate drumbeat and the soulful sound of the pipes reminded us of the service and the sacrifice that defines our noble profession.

My mind wandered to the terrible events on that fateful day. When terrorists hit the two towers our country was plunged into a depth of despair and depression that had not been seen in many years. The strike on the towers not only activated, but also united our people to fight a common enemy. I can't remember such patriotism and sense of purpose since the years of the Second World War. It made me very sad at the great loss of life, but at the same time very proud to be an American.

That fateful day and some of the days that followed, I was so choked up that I found it hard to talk to anyone about events of that day. I kept thinking about the many, many fire fighters, police officers and rescue personnel who rushed up the stairs to help the injured and assist in evacuating the buildings. I had climbed fire escapes in multi-story buildings many times and I knew full well what they were feeling.

Hundreds of good young men and women desperately trying to do their jobs only to have a massive building collapse, extinguishing their young lives and burying them under tons of debris. The dastardly and depraved act on September 11 so affected me as a retired fire fighter that I was in a daze for days. Our nation, likewise, suffered emotionally as it assessed the events of that awful day.

Our leaders of the United States, the leaders of New York and every other city in our great nation stood together in trying to make sense of our tragedy. The people were united, and retribution was decisively extracted. Fire and rescue teams from throughout the country were sent to assist in rescue and recovery efforts. The San Antonio Fire Department assisted by sending a rescue team to this horrific scene.

The year 2001 can be considered a tragic year because of the great loss of life of so many innocent people; however, 2001 was also a good year in that it brought out the best in people. Unity, courtesies, respect, helpfulness and a sincere concern for fellow Americans were abundant and could readily be seen and felt in our everyday life.

When collections were taken up at street corners, our citizens couldn't give enough. They dug deep into their pockets and sometimes gave more than they could really afford. Gold rings, watches, religious medals, silver and gold chains and some gold coins were put in the boots of firefighters who were taking up collections at street corners.

During the walk from Milam Square to the Alamo, people along the sidewalks clapped and cheered as the solemn procession of fire fighters and first responders passed. I thought to myself what an impression we could have made with two or three times the number of fire fighters and first responders. How fitting it would have been if all off duty fire fighters had participated in this memorial. It could have been a tremendous show of respect and an honor to all our fallen brothers and sisters. It would have also shown the unity of our extended fire fighting family.

Now more than ever we should be united. We should be proud of our work as fire fighters, police officers, paramedics and first responders. Let's stand together and never forget our brothers and sisters who gave their all, in defense of humanity. We must forever continue to remember those who came before us and laid the groundwork for our proud and noble professions.

We will never forget.

Fraternally,

Henry Trevino

Reflections: One of the noblest acts of man is to come to the defense of one who is unable to defend himself. It takes great courage to put your life on the line to protect and shield a person that you may not even know. Bravery defines a person who has the courage to stand up and fight at all costs, even to the point of dying, for what is right. A hero is no braver than an ordinary man, the difference is that he is brave 5 minutes longer. – Henry Trevino

Living With Anxiety Disorder

So I tell you, when you pray for something, believe that you have already received it. Then it will be yours. Mark 11:24

I vividly remember my first one. I was around 11 years old, at a football game with my best friend. Her older brother was playing and we had gone with her parents. I was sitting in the bleachers listening to all the cheering and people screaming. All of a sudden, it appeared to come out of nowhere. I felt weird. It was a feeling I had never felt before, at least not that intense. My heart started beating extremely fast and I was hot despite the fact that it was chilly outside. I felt nauseated with an intense urge to run and cry.

I told my friend that I needed to go to the bathroom. The bathrooms were in this little brick outhouse that barely had doors. My friend followed, struggling to keep up with me. Once I got to the stall I let go. I fell to the ground and sobbed. I remember my whole body shaking. My friend and her mom kept asking me what was wrong, and I had no idea how to answer. All I knew was that I had to get of there and be with my mom. I felt so embarrassed and ashamed that I was a middle school girl crying for her mom. That is how it all started. My downward spiral of panic attacks and generalized anxiety disorder only got worse.

I wish I could say I did my time, suffered my attacks, found a magic pill and I am cured now. I am far from anxiety free, but I have come a long way. It has been a very long, scary and expensive battle. All through middle school and high school I tried so many different things to help myself. My poor mom did not know what to do with me. She tried her very best to get self-help books, tapes, online programs, coaching phone calls, and several therapists. Back then anxiety was not publicly discussed. People were ashamed to have this disorder, or at least I know I was.

Some of the years were a blur. Some of the years I was perfectly fine because for whatever reason my anxiety was kept at bay. Then other years it would hit me hard. While in high school, I remember waking up some mornings, so anxious that I would end up on the bathroom floor, shaking and crying.

The thought of living my life with these overwhelming, scary and terrorizing feelings almost convinced me that I didn't want to go on. I always felt like I was different from my friends. Like I was trapped. I was not free to do things I really wanted to do. I was so scared I would have a panic attack in front of people, and that would just be the worst thing that could happen at my age. My disorder kept me from so many opportunities I would have loved to experience but could not because of my fear. I had opportunities to travel abroad, try out for the dance team at school, go on trips with friends. I would not even ride in a car with anyone, unless I was driving.

This disorder collided really hard with my personality. I loved being in the popular group; the "in" crowd, doing what everyone else was doing. I became known for being a "phobia," not showing up for gatherings or parties which I had every intention of going to; until I would get hit with another anxiety attack. It was so difficult to plan things, to do things I wanted to do, that I often questioned if it was even worth it. I could never seem to relieve myself of this heavy weight that constantly pulled me away from doing the things I knew I really wanted to.

When I was 21, I remember going to bars and parties, with my key in my pocket, in case I had to make a run for it. There were times I would be in line for the bathroom on the brink of having an anxiety attack, worrying about whether I would make it through to the front of the line. I would try my hardest to do the things my tapes and therapist suggested, like self-talk and "float with the feeling not fight it." But my feelings were so intense that those things would not work for me. I couldn't concentrate on conversations my friends and I would be having, because I was so consumed with trying to prevent the dreaded panic attack. When my anxiety was high which was more often than not, I never really felt present. I was always thinking of the worst-case scenario and what I would do if it came to that. I constantly lived in the future of the "what ifs."

I remember the day I "gave in." I was either a sophomore or junior in college. I was with my "then" boyfriend that I had been together with for a couple of years. He knew everything I was going through. One day, my brother was having a get together at his house. We both wanted to go and were excited. About an hour before we were supposed to leave, out of nowhere, an overwhelming feeling of dread consumed my entire being. I had no specific reason why. I remember sitting on the bed with my boyfriend and told him, *"I can't go and I can't keep living like this."*

I always knew medication was an option for this type of issue, but I never thought I could do it. It was mostly frowned upon if you went down to that level. I felt like if I had to take medication, something was seriously wrong with me or I was crazy. This was going on for about 8-9 years that I had been living with this nightmare. I felt like I had tried everything other than medication. But enough was enough. So, there I went, to my first physiatrist, with my tail between my legs feeling completely ashamed.

"Some people have anxiety; some people have an anxiety disease; some people need medication the way you would need it if you had heart or blood problems." This is what my doctor told me that made me see things a little differently. I finally tried medication for the first time. It was through trial and error that I found the medication that seemed to lift some of the heavy weight I had been

carrying, for so many years. I began to feel enough relief to do and practice some of the things my books and therapist had taught me. I also found a therapist within the same practice that I saw weekly that really helped me.

I am by no means saying to go get medication if you suffer from anxiety. I am just sharing my story. Every person is different and responds to treatments in a different way. I am not saying I am anxiety free by any means. I am saying I know what it feels like to live with a life hindering condition and then through trial and error finding a way out. I am saying that for me, my life has changed since I started my medication, found the right fit therapist, and began depending more on God.

I no longer feel like I can't handle life. I no longer feel like it is such hard work just to get through the day. I have more energy and mind space to do and think about other things in life. I can ride in cars with others now, not always having to drive, I go on trips with friends, and enjoy things I have never been able to do before. Sure, my panic sneaks back up on me sometimes, but it is not every single minute of every single day.

I think people who struggle with heavy anxiety will always have it, to an extent. It is just part of who you are, perhaps something in your genes. But it is about finding the right combination of treatment that allows you to live a good quality life. I remember the words of my doctor, *"You need to decide if you want a better- quality life and if that means taking medication, then that's what you need to do."* I would love to one day be medication free, but that might not ever happen, and I am ok with that now. It has been over ten years since I first walked into the physiatrist's office. It has been and probably always will be a roller coaster of good and bad months. But I know now there is always a light at the end of the tunnel.

I am so grateful that through my struggles God has been with me. I know that I could not have survived on my own. I am grateful for the constant love and support of my family and friends. So, now, when the ugly face of anxiety wants to disrupt my life, I ask for God to help me handle it. It is a very big obstacle, but not bigger than what God is able to do for me. – *Natalie Hart*

Reflection: You can say that I truly lived through hell. The fears that I have experienced taught me that I am strong and that I can live through whatever life gives me. I know that I could not have survived by myself. God, our creator was with me every step of the way. With each new day that God blessed me, he also provided me the power to survive. – Henry Trevino

Love And Devotion

In the same way, the Holy Spirit helps us when we are weak. We don't know what we should pray for. But the Spirit himself prays for us. He prays through groans too deep for words. Romans 8:26

When you know someone as long as I've known Daniel, (Danny), my lover, my husband and my rock of Gibraltar, you can say that we really are stalwart and best of friends. Danny and I have been together for over 40 years. You go through life comfortable with each other and you tend to grow complacent with your relationship. That complacency was severely tested in the days that followed our Easter dinner celebration

Easter Monday, March 22, 2008, Danny proved his love and his great devotion to the children and me. The children had come to our home to enjoy our Easter dinner. We always enjoyed holidays with our kids and some of our very close friends. Our children, my son Daniel Izaak and his wife Mari and our daughter Rebekah arrived right on time to help set the table. Our Easter morning started with great expectations of a joyful dinner.

As we all pitched in and started to prepare the food and set the table, I suddenly felt something was not right. It started slowly at first; suddenly it devolved into the worst headache of my whole life. It hit me like a ton of bricks; it was blinding; something I had never experienced.

My dear Danny and my children got me dressed and put me in the car. We had a very fast drive to the Medical Center. Danny and my daughter knew that I was in excruciating pain. I don't remember anything that happened just before we got to the hospital; I was completely out of connection with the real world. For days I was completely in a fog unknowing what was happening around me. It was days after when I found out about all the details that occurred during my crisis.

The Methodist emergency room personal must have been hopping because they saved my life. I woke up days later in the ICU, (Intensive Care Unit). I was diagnosed with an extremely serious subarachnoid aneurism. They told me that I had been saved by the very fast action of the emergency unit personnel, the right procedures and by a very talented and capable doctor.

The doctors used a new coiling procedure that sealed the bleeding from the inside. They stopped the bleeding by threading the coiling device through my femoral artery to apply the glue. It was a very serious procedure with a low probability of success. The doctors gave my husband, Danny, no expectations or possibility of success. I eventually recovered from the delicate procedure that the doctors orchestrated in saving my life. My family was always at my side during the three of four months of convalescence and physical therapy.

Prior to my crises with the ruptured aneurism I had been working as a teacher at Saint Anthony elementary school. During my convalescence my students, their families and the school staff were extremely supportive during this medical situation. I received flowers, notes and a lot of love from many of my friends.

I continued my recovery, which I didn't think was going fast enough. I didn't have much loss of physical function; however, I did lose my ability in my math skills. Recovery was like starting school all over again. I suffered from aphasia which effects word recognition. There are certain degrees of aphasia; luckily, I was not seriously affected to a large degree. I remember that I could see the word, but I could not say the word. It was very frustrating to have this condition.

My cognitive ability has recovered to a very great degree; however, I still struggle with math. I found a way to circumvent this deficiency; I'm glad someone invented calculators. They were lifesavers for me.

Having to readjust and relearn certain functions caused me to go through some mental depression. This lasted for a short time. Once school started all my faculties continued to improve, slowly but steadily. I continued teaching for two more years. By this time, I had been teaching for 34 years. I finally decided to retire in 2010.

I thought that it was time to give myself and my family priority after such a long ordeal. I continue to reminisce about how lucky I was to overcome my disabilities and continue to teach. Many of my students still come back to tell me of their success in school, their accomplishments and their triumphs. I consider myself very lucky to have been able to teach the children of many of my previous students. I feel very happy that they have lived a life inspired by my teaching and guidance.

My husband, Danny retired in 2011 from the San Antonio Police Department. He was given a retirement party by his friends, family and all the police brothers. We even invited peer teachers from school to make it a double retirement celebration.

Since our retirement we have taken a couple of wonderful vacations together. We went to Europe in 2015 and saw Paris, Venice and a lot of Germany. We took a cruise in 2016 to Mazatlán, Grand Cayman Islands and Jamaica. I can truly say that I have lived my life to the fullest. I have no regrets or doubts of how lucky I was to have recovered from a very serious medical emergency. I know that God has been by my side my whole life. How else can I explain my good fortune with my life surrounded by my family and my many very good friends? – *Maggie Valdez*

Reflections: Without doubt the best medicine is the closeness of a friend, the lending of an ear, the holding of a hand or praying with a person going through a serious illness. The skill of the physicians, the love of a husband, and the closeness of the family is undoubtedly due to the intervention of our Almighty God. God's word is absolute; pray to him, recognize his unwavering love and his intercession in time of great need. – Henry Trevino

Loving Dedication to the End

My dear brothers and sisters, remain strong in the faith. Don't let anything move you. Always give yourselves completely to the work of the Lord. Because you belong to the Lord, you know that your work is not worthless. 1 Corinthians 15:58

If we are so blessed to have our parents in our lives well into their older years, it is likely that we may be called on to assist them in varying degrees with their daily lives. Depending on where one is in their life, sometimes the caregiving of our loved one can fall more on one who's circumstances allow it; but as a child of our parent and a child of God, we must willingly accept what God would have us do, as difficult as it might be.

After 25 years of service at Dillard's Corp as a traffic manager, I was notified that the San Antonio office would be closing its operation. Although all the executive officers were offered positions to other locations outside of San Antonio, it was just not going to work for me. I was even given the opportunity to go to Mexico City and help open a new store. The advantage I had over other qualified persons was the fact that they preferred someone who was bilingual.

Unfortunately, I was not able to accept any transfer outside of San Antonio because of my obligation to my mother. My husband had died in 1992, my children were grown and therefore I decided to retire and help take care of my mother, whose health had been slowly declining. My other siblings either lived out of state or were still working fulltime. I was the most logical one to take over the responsibility.

My siblings and I did hire a wonderful lady who stayed with her when none of us were able to, but as the primary caregiver, I needed to go every day and see that all was well and provide whatever my mother needed. My brothers and sister would do what they could after work and on weekends.

Over time our mother began declining in her physical sickness as well as her mental state. Not only did she need more help with just getting around, but also it got to the point, where she became fearful of everyone and everything. She couldn't recognize others, or remember if she had eaten or not, or whether she had taken her meds. I guess her being fearful of everything, caused her to refuse to take her meds when we tried to administer them to her and bathing her also became a major confrontation. She was very modest and insisted that either my sister or I had to be present to help with her baths.

As the months passed, we all needed to spend even more time with her. The daily visits became all day visits, which gradually became overnight stays. Even though we had a caregiver to help, one of her children had to be present around the clock.

Taking care of her and providing for her needs became more intense, more time consuming and overwhelming. My heart ached for her when everything had to be done for her. She had to be fed, her arms and legs had to be moved and flexed and turned in bed every hour. It became a real struggle to give her medications, change her and bathe her.

On May 9th, 1997 everything changed. I was on my way to my mother's house and was involved in a car accident. My first thought was, *"How will I be able to take care of my mother now?"* She needed me, and I felt useless in not being able to do all the things I had been helping her with.

I was in severe pain all over my body for at least a month. I tried not to think about it, as the only thing I was concerned about was my mother. During this time, I continued to visit her every day, but not without feelings of frustration, anger and guilt that I couldn't do all the things that she relied on me for. I was still grateful that I was able to at least comfort her by continuously holding her hand and to reassure her that I was present with her.

Our darling mother passed away peacefully in November 1998 at the age of 94. I was exactly where God wanted me to be, beside her holding her hand. I since had come to accept and forgive myself for the times I couldn't help her physically after my accident. But I am grateful for my husband and family who supported me when I needed them. They were by my side through this difficult time. And because of their love for me, it gave me much comfort that I was with my mother in her last days. Thank you, God, for when you came for my mother, you gently carried her away from out of my hand, into yours. – *Mary Louise Trevino*

Reflection: The woman called mother is the seed who gave us life. She is the root that nourishes and makes us strong. A mother is willing to sacrifice everything including her life for her loved ones. Never will you be forsaken nor ignored by your mother. Your mother has taught you how to love, how to be tender, gentle and kindhearted. – Henry Trevino

Motherly Love

I prayed for this child, and the Lord has granted me what I asked of him. 1 Samuel 1:27

Ron and I were married in 1971 in Newington, Connecticut where I had lived all my life. I was the second oldest of seven children, six girls and one boy. I lived at home until I got married at the very young age of 29. Ron, being 12 years older than me, loved to hear that he "robbed the cradle."

We, of course wanted a family, so after two years and a few medical tests that were inconclusive, we decided to look into adoption. After talking to several adoption agencies and being told that, Ron and I were too old, or we hadn't been married long enough, we eventually found an agency here in San Antonio that would at least allow us to attend an open meeting. This was in November 1974. Three months later, a social worker by the name of Lisa, placed our daughter Julie in our arms.

Julie was born one year to the month after we put in our papers for her adoption; she was truly a blessing. In those times, extensive detailed information on her birth parents was not available, so we really knew nothing about them. Our prayer, each day since then, has been one of being grateful that our daughter's birth mother chose to give her life. Our wish would be that somehow, she knew how grateful we were.

I was fortunate to stay home with our daughter for the first 3 years of her life. She brought us so much joy watching her grow into a sweet and loving little girl. Over time she became a talented singer and ballerina. We were very proud and blessed parents.

During her middle school years, we noticed that she began showing an excessive amount of anger, resentment and low self-esteem. My husband and I struggled as we did our best to implement our parenting skills. We finally made the decision to seek professional counseling for all of us. Back then, seeking counseling was very private and something we didn't feel comfortable sharing with family and friends.

Aside from the usual teenage struggles, at one point during her freshman year, she informed me that she had been raped. While in counseling, we unfortunately received and heeded some very bad advice. We were discouraged from reporting the rape and were told that we would "make things worse" and to "let it go." After this episode our daughter's behavior, attitude, feelings and outlook worsened daily. She even ran away a few times for two or three days at a time, which was pure hell for my husband and me.

It was the summer after her freshman year that a psychologist recommended that we should intervene more vigorously at this point. We admitted her to a psychiatric hospital. She remained there the entire summer and continued her schooling there as a day student until the second semester of her sophomore year. Upon her release from the hospital she was enrolled in a catholic school and did very well until the end of the school year. Unfortunately, Julie continued on the wrong path of a self-abusive, self-destructive way of life to the point that she was asked to leave the school.

I eventually became tougher than I ever imagined I could be. I told Julie that she was welcome to visit when we were home, she was welcome to share a meal with us but she was not welcome to stay in our home for any length of time until she could live by our house rules. She immediately put me on a guilt trip even though I felt like I was doing what was best for her. I prayed constantly that God would take care of her. I kept my sanity by envisioning a band of angels hovering around her, one of them being my dad.

In 1993, Julie informed us that she was pregnant and would deliver in January of 94. The birth father was only a casual relationship, so she was going to parent this baby by herself with help from her "friends." After praying to God for guidance, we told our daughter that in spite of the fact that we loved her and the baby, we would not help her parent the baby. Obviously, we felt that the baby needed two stable loving parents.

During this time while she was pregnant, she did move back in with us. It was difficult for me at first. I was shocked at my feelings. I really didn't want her in our home. I wanted to find a home where she could stay. My anger, disappointment, resentment and frustration were overwhelming. I could not understand or explain why I was feeling this way. I prayed to God to soften my heart, and to help me to be happy that my daughter was here and to embrace and enjoy the time I had with her.

We continued our counseling sessions, which Julie also attended. Again, after much thought and prayer, Julie decided that she would place her baby for adoption. She began to shop around and eventually found some agencies that offered some wonderful financial help while she was pregnant. One condition on the adoption was that she would not have any information on where her baby would be placed.

Julie continued her search for other adoption agencies because she definitely wanted an open adoption. Seemingly out of nowhere, our longtime counselor who had helped since Julie's hospitalization, intervened and convinced her that he had a friend who worked for an agency in San Antonio that he was sure could help her. Julie trusted him so he invited both of them to his office to discuss the adoption.

I drove her to his office that day and although she wanted me to go with her, I knew she had to make the decision herself. When she and the social worker came out together, I was shocked and dumbfounded to see Lisa, the very same worker who had placed Julie with us. Lisa was now working for a different agency, which provided open adoptions. Wow! It was amazing to me how God's plan was unfolding. Julie said that when she met Lisa, and Lisa learned what her last name was, Julie was informed of the connection. Julie did select her child's adoptive parents ahead of time, so she was able to establish a trusting relationship with them.

I prayed extremely hard to be able to get back to being happy my daughter was o.k. and to enjoy the time I had with her. Happily, I became her labor coach. What an experience. Never having experienced a pregnancy myself, I really did enjoy learning about everything having to do with a pregnancy. I was privileged to be an active part of my granddaughter's birth. I didn't realize for a long time, that during Julie's pregnancy, God was helping me heal, and not only preparing me to love and help my granddaughter into this world, but also to support my daughter in placing her baby daughter with her adoptive parents.

I had the privilege of cradling our precious granddaughter for an hour only minutes after she was born. Believing she could hear the feeling in my voice without understanding the words, I tried to tell her how much I loved her; how much we all loved her. My heart overflowed with emotions that I was unable to verbalize. I held her little form close to me, gently kissing her soft pink cheeks and tiny, perfect ears, traced the outline of her small lips, and stroked the peach fuzz on her fragile little head and said to my dearest granddaughter:

"My heart is filled with pride, sadness, excitement, longing and a never-ending supply of love. It hurts that due to circumstances; you will be a part of another family. Your wonderful birth-mother, (my daughter) is giving you selflessly, the most valuable and precious thing she can give you – loving, caring, stable and capable parents who have prayed for you for a very long time. The most beautiful thing I've heard your birth mother say is something she will tell you at the placement service that will come only too soon. Before she places you in the arms of the people whom God meant you to be with, she will say these bittersweet words; 'I'm not leaving you, I'm letting you grow.' We will always love you. Our love for you began as you began your life inside your mother. You were conceived and born for a reason – a very special purpose."

In 1995 Julie again was pregnant in what she thought was a good relationship. She moved in with the birthfather's family. When the baby was born, she and the baby's father separated, and Julie and the baby moved in with us. Julie, I am proud to say had become a wonderful parent, in spite of the negative feelings she still harbored about herself. Three years later, Julie had another baby boy.

God does answer prayers according to his plans, which at times I forget. It was in the summer of 2000; Julie met her husband who was truly a gift. They encountered many obstacles and challenges along the way, yet they were so blessed and had become better partners and parents. He was a very good and faithful husband and a great father to his two boys. Unfortunately, he died in 2004 at the very young age of 24 from an overdose of pain medication and other over the counter drugs.

My dear daughter, Julie never fully recovered from her psychological problems, difficulties and the loss of her husband after only three years of marriage. She passed away in 2007 at the age of

33. She died alone and depressed in the lonely room where she lived. The cause of death was from an overdose of drugs.

Julie's baby girl is now grown up, working and living out of state. Her second son is now working and living in San Antonio. He is married and is now the proud father of a beautiful baby girl. Julie's third and youngest son is a husky, tall, beautiful young man. He lives with me, his grandmother, and is still going to school. He will be graduating in another two years. He is a whiz with computers. Hopefully he will be able to use those skills when he finishes his studies.

My husband, Ron passed away in 2002 from a ruptured aneurism. He was a dear man and I still miss him very much. I miss his love, his smile, his guidance and his friendship. I am grateful for my grandchildren and how we have all remained connected. I continue to thank God for the many years of life he has given me. My faith and strong belief in God helped me survive and heal from the many tragedies that crossed my path. As hard and difficult as life is, God in his infinite wisdom and mercy got me through those dark days and I know that I was never alone. – *Anonymous*

Reflection: Remember the adage of one set of footsteps in the sand. God said, "My dear child; it was during your times of trial and suffering, when you see only one set of footprints, it was then that I carried you." – Henry Trevino

My Battle With Cancer

Give a lot of time and effort to prayer. Always be watchful and thankful. Colossians 4:2

February 2017 was the day that changed my life. I went to the Fire and Police clinic for my six-month physical. I went through the regular exam and then asked the doctor for a PSA. The doctor did not think it was necessary, however, at my insistence he drew some blood.

To my surprise the doctor called me 2 days later; he seemed perplexed, and asked *"So, what the hell is going on with your prostate? Your PSA is at 10.8! I'm going to get you in to see a urologist."* The clinic doctor explained that generally there was no pain from cancer in the prostate; however, once the cancer has spread from the prostate to other parts of the body there could be severe pain. Once it spreads into the bones, bladder and other organs discomfort and pain can become a real problem.

I was directed to a urologist that the clinic doctor suggested. A biopsy was done, 12 cores were removed from the prostate. Within a few days the urologist called and after a brief meeting he recommended a prostatectomy; it would be by robotic surgery. The procedure was state of the art and the latest use of robotics in prostatectomy surgery. The procedure would cause minimal down time and I would be cancer free.

The doctor's advice was a relief after hearing the word CANCER. The surgery was scheduled a couple of months later; however, in the meantime I felt it necessary to get a second opinion. I showed the next urologist the finding from the biopsy and he concurred; he agreed that the prostate had to be removed. The doctor went on to say; *"I can get you in on a Saturday; I do about 15 in a day."*

I was feeling leery about this second opinion, so I sought a third opinion from a third doctor. The doctor said that he could get me in for the operation as soon as possible, but with sobering consequences. I would be impotent, and I would be incontinent for an unknown amount of time and with no guarantee that any proper function would return. The thought of wearing pullups and never having intimacy again was worse than the cancer.

The other doctors had spoken very little about the permanent side effects. The first doctor said there might be a little problem with impotence, however, whenever I wanted intimacy, he could give me an injection directly into the penis and I could possibly be able to function. The sad part about prostatectomy is that in many cases the cancer returns to many who have this type surgery. After being advised by three doctors that an operation was the only way to go it seemed that I had no choice; I turned to God and asked for his mercy and his guidance.

Countless hours of researching lead me to M.D. Anderson hospital in Houston where they have treatments called proton therapy. There are only 2 hospitals in Texas that have this, Dallas and Houston. There are maybe 10 proton centers in the United States and 15 in the world. It is not really new; it's been around for 9 years. It is not experimental, and Medicare covers it. While I was doing my research, I learned quite a bit about prostate cancer. I found out that one in seven men would be diagnosed with prostate cancer. The majority of these men will have an unnecessary prostatectomy that will change their life forever.

I applied online to M.D. Anderson Hospital; within 3 hours a nurse called me back and asked a lot of questions. She requested the entire test results from the doctors that I had seen in San Antonio. In about a week a doctor called me and asked me to come to Houston to be evaluated. I returned to Houston about 3 times and was finally accepted into the program. What is proton therapy? Proton therapy is an advanced form of radiation treatment that delivers a powerful highly precise beam of radiation directly into the tumor. It is precise; it spares healthy tissue, decreases both short- and long-term side effects and improves quality of life. The stress and headaches caused from trying to find a place in Houston to live for 2 months was overwhelming. Luckily, the time was cut short by Bobby Ford and Shane George. They advised me to go to Rotary Firefighter Home. The IAFF and Rotary International have partnered up to provide a home for first responders and their families who suffer from cancer.

You are your own best advocate. If something doesn't seem right, if you don't feel you're getting the right, answers move on! The men I met having this therapy all found out about it with their own research. Some of the men that I met at the hospital were being treated for cancer after having their prostate removed. They were so angry because they have been incontinent and impotent for years. The advice they received was; complete removal of the prostate.

It's now been two months since my last treatment and I am physically returning to normal. While my body functions are getting better, I will continue to be monitored for a few years to be sure the cancer is held in check. Every day I thank and pray to the Lord and the doctors that treated me. I firmly believe that prayer had a prominent positive effect psychologically and physically.

I ask all of my first responder friends to consider this organization, rotaryfirefighterhome.org the next time they donate to a charity. It could be you or your family that might need their help in the future. They provided me a 1-bedroom apartment fully furnished for 2 months and a onetime cleaning cost of $125.00. The generosity that was accorded me, plus the many friends I made along the way were a true God sent. I was very lucky with my battle with cancer. I have no doubt that God guided me in the right direction the whole time.

I felt it my duty to inform you of my personal experience. This gives me the opportunity to strongly advice you not to let the worry and anxiety keep you from getting a physical exam every six months.
– *Frank Wilborn*

Reflection: God will always be there to hold your hand and comfort you in time of need. He will never forsake you or abandon you when you desperately need his love and his friendship. Many unexplained miracles occur every day. Sometimes they don't occur right away, but that doesn't mean that God is not listening. Continue your prayers and miracles will happen; the important thing is not to give up on God. – Henry Trevino

My Dad's Truck

Forget the things that happened in the past. Do not keep on thinking about them. I am about to do something new. It is beginning to happen even now. Don't you see it coming? Isaiah 43:18-19

Sometimes we are led to do things; perhaps out of character, by a gentle nudge we can't explain, or maybe a force from within that seems to make no sense. If we open our hearts and minds and allow the experience to flow naturally, we may receive a blessing, witness a miracle or get to a place of peace and acceptance by the mere act of letting go. We position ourselves on the front line to allow God to prompt us to go in the direction He wants us to follow or to acquire the lessons He wishes us to learn. Perhaps, it's to find a purpose or meaning that if ignored, would be a missed opportunity to experience the wonderment of a miraculous event.

I know some people wondered why I would take a job selling cars. Yes, to put it more bluntly, "used cars." For three days, I was a "used car salesman." I wasn't particularly looking for a job; I didn't even think I wanted one. But, if you have ever heard the saying, *"It just fell in my lap,"* that pretty much describes how it all happened.

The day I walked into Car Max, I was looking for a truck, not a job. Little did I know at the time, that God not only showed me the truck He wanted me to have, but He also had something else lined up for me that took me clearly by surprise.

God had already put things in motion even before I arrived at the dealer. My truck, which used to be my dad's, was full of junk that I was going to take to the dumpster after helping my son Daniel move from his apartment to his new house. The bed of the truck was full of stuff, mostly old pieces of wood and particleboard.

The salesman who assisted me suggested that he take the truck to the back and have it appraised. I looked at the junk that I had intended to take to the dumpster before I was sidetracked. He told me not to worry about it; he would take care of everything and it would not affect the price of the appraisal in any way.

The truck that God wanted me to have was a shiny red Ford F150. Because of the excitement and how pleased I was with the transaction, it dawned on me that my old truck was now gone. My truck that used to be dads, the one I never really had wanted to get rid of for sentimental reasons, was out of sight and I thought out of mind.

In my conversation with the salesman, who was also part of God's plan, informed me that they were hiring and asked if I would like to work there. He suggested I put in an application as he went on and on about how nice of a place it was to work at. I had done a lot of business there in the past, everyone was very nice, and I liked the atmosphere. So, I thought, *"Why not?"*

That evening I filled out my application online, they interviewed me immediately and pretty much hired me on the spot. Before I knew it, even before I had time to think about it, I was hired. I would be starting the next week with a couple of weeks of training, and then after that I would be working about 20 hours a week; on weeknights and some Saturdays.

It dawned on me that I had accepted a job that I didn't really want or need for that matter. But still for reasons I wouldn't know until later, I had this willingness to go along. I felt a sense of urgency that it was just something I needed to do. It was not something that aligned with the way I felt about work. As I've gotten older my philosophy has always been to work less than the previous year and yet make more money, spend more time with family and put in more tee times. Yet I was determined to see how this was going to unfold.

The first day of training came and went and all was fine. It was on the second day in which the natural flow of events became out of the ordinary in the life of a salesman in training. For reasons only God knew at the time, I was pulled from my training and asked to help out in another department where they needed help.

On Tuesdays, there at Car Max, they auction off the cars and trucks that for whatever reason will not be sold on the lot. That particular day, there were about 100 cars and trucks that were on the auctioning block. By the time I arrived to help, they had already gone through about 50. My job was to help others drive each car through this barn where it is showed for people to begin bidding.

It was the second car that I was assigned to drive through, that startled me. It was my old truck; my dad's truck, the one I thought I was never going to see again. As I drove that truck through the barn, I initially looked in the back somewhat embarrassed by the junk that was still there. But that junk was part of the miracle. As I drove to the front of the barn, it occurred to me what the significance of everything meant.

As the people began bidding, the little lump in my throat that had been there for the last 2 ½ years swelled up and burst in a matter of seconds as the tears began running down my cheeks. I had not cried since the death of my dad. I pictured my dad at the pearly gates being welcomed with open arms just the way he was. Just like the people bidding on my dad's truck, junk and all. They wanted it, with whatever dents and scratches it had acquired over time.

Daddy was in essence telling me to let him go. He was fine, he was happy, and he was loved in the most perfect world. All of his sins had been forgiven and he wanted me to love and forgive also. He was giving me permission to not only let him go, but also all of the extra baggage he had accumulated in his life on earth. I needed to let go of regrets, hurts, apologies never made, words spoken, and words unspoken. I cannot put into words the relief I felt with that release of "letting go." I grieved for the loss of my dad and also at the tears of joy in knowing that he was still alive in a bigger and better way.

I thanked Car Max for the role they played, and they thanked me for sharing it with them. Things unfolded exactly the way they were supposed to. Every minute, every detail was aligned in perfect order. There is no way something so big could have been planned in such great detail on my own. Call it a gut feeling, a higher power or inner guide; it was something greater than myself that moved me every step of the way.

This was something I did not do on my own. I didn't question it even though it didn't make sense. I followed Gods' lead; I allowed His guidance to direct my path even though I had no idea where I was going. I do know that daddy had a hand in all of this. Those three days on that job were not a coincidence; it was all predestined to come to light.

Some of the most intimate and best times I spent with daddy were the days we spent at the cattle auctions. Although this was a car auction it came with a significant meaning which only he and I understood. I never expected something so big to come out of something so "not me." But that's the way miracles happen. They come when you least expect them; in ways you never would've imagined'

I hope that by sharing my story, you will not only experience miracles of your own, but that you will come to expect them. Thank you Car Max for hiring me and releasing me three days later. I also thank the most important man in my life; my daddy for helping me see the light and I thank you God for being that "Light." – *Pete Leal*

Reflection: We must learn to accept what is now, let go of what was, and have faith in what will be. Life will continue to evolve and pass into the land of memories. We must be thankful and accept the passing of time and the chapters of our life. The many memories created with our loved ones will not allow us to forget the many past events in our life. Continue to visit the land of memories but also allow yourself to continue to live in the present and dream of the future. – Henry Trevino

My Journey During Dialysis

Don't let your heart be troubled. Believe in God. Believe also in me. John 14:1

The year was 2004; I went in for a checkup with my family doctor in Laredo, Texas. After running tests, he explained to me that my protein levels were not normal and referred me to a local nephrologist. The specialist ordered more tests and when we sat down to review the results he said without any hesitation *"I have to start you on dialysis."* I was shocked! My immediate response was *"I would like to get a second opinion."* He complied with my request and I feel to this day that I made the right decision.

My sister, Leti is a nurse in San Antonio, Texas. I asked her to give us a recommendation for a nephrologist and that is how Dr. Melissa Isbell was put in my path. On my first visit, I immediately felt comfortable with her. My husband, Servando, and I were comforted by how knowledgeable she seemed to be in her field and felt she would help me through this.

Her diagnosis was IgA nephropathy, which is an autoimmune disease that affects the filters of the kidneys. IgA is an immunoglobulin, which is a part of an individual's healthy immune system. A defective form of IgA molecule attaches itself to another IgA molecule instead of an infection, causing an immune complex.

Dr. Isbell flat out told me, *"You will eventually be on dialysis, but it's up to you when that will start."* I asked her, *"What do you mean?"* She explained to me that I would need to make a lifestyle change and follow her treatment plan. Under my doctors' care, my hard work and by the grace of God, I was able to stay off dialysis for 11 years. I often wonder where I would be if I had started dialysis when I was originally told I needed it so long ago.

During one of my routine visits, my doctor proceeded to ask me the usual questions that she asked me every time I went to see her. *"Are you having any headaches, do you get out of breath, do you have bouts of diarrhea, are you throwing up, are you swelling more?"* In all my other visits the answers were always *"No."* To my surprise, I answered yes to all her questions. What came next was inevitable. Dr. Isbell looked at me and said, *"It is time for dialysis."* My heart sank and I began crying. Of course, I was grateful for all the extra time I was given in which I managed to stay on top of this disease, but still I was not prepared to hear those words again. I realized that my life was going to become very challenging and a lot harder by having to be on dialysis, I prayed to God for his help. *"Oh Lord my God, in you I put my trust."*

The type of dialysis my doctor prescribed was Peritoneal or PD. PD is less invasive and stressful on the body and could be done at home. In preparation for this, a catheter was surgically placed in my abdomen. My husband Servando and I had to go through five weeks of extensive training to learn how to properly administer my treatments; both automatically with a dialysis machine, and manually involving an IV pole, in the event of having no electricity due to storms etc. Both options were to remove deadly toxins building up in my body.

During those five weeks, my sister Leti and brother-in-law Jorge, generously let us stay at their home, which we will always be grateful for. We were comforted knowing that they would play a big part in supporting me through my journey and they would help us both come back to God. While we were there, we noticed their devotion to God and their spiritual faith. We witnessed how they lived and loved so effortlessly. We realized that we had to open up our hearts and find that same spiritual faith. We wanted what they had.

One day out of nowhere, my sister Leti noticed my depression was getting the best of me so she gently grabbed my arm and said, *"Let's go."* *"Go where?"* I asked. She just repeated, *"Let's go, and just get in the car."* We ended up at church. As I got down on my knees and began praying, I immediately felt Gods' presence. My tears began falling, which turned into crying, which turned into an explosive outburst that seemed to last forever. It was what my body and my heart needed. I firmly believe this was an important turning point for me.

I realized during this time how other people in my life were making sacrifices. After the five weeks of training at the dialysis clinic was over, I then had to come back for one week out of every month. My sister Beatriz Gloria offered one of her extra bedrooms for my use. She never once complained about the extra baggage that had to come along with me; boxes of solution, drain bags, IV pole, and other supplies, plus clothes and luggage for my husband and me.

I also realized how much of what I was going through was not just my journey, but also all the people who loved me. My husband was the one who witnessed most of my anger and yet he never left my side or complained. God gave him the courage and strength to become a loving caregiver in spite of this new life I had thrust on him. Looking back, I feel almost ashamed that I failed to notice how wonderful my husband was to me during this time.

During the year and a half while I was on dialysis, I was overwhelmed with so many emotions. In the beginning I was filled with anger. I felt that my life was over. It didn't help when I would run into people or they would come to visit and say the words, *"I'm sorry."* To me I took that to mean that I was going to be on dialysis for the rest of my life or perhaps I was going to die soon. I didn't want to die yet, so I began having bouts of depression, sometimes just wanting to give up.

I was registered with UNOS (United Network for Organ sharing), as an option to get a live donor. My mother wanted desperately to give me one of her kidneys, as any mother would do for her child. Unfortunately, she was not a good match due to her age and that was so disappointing for her. I have seven brothers and sisters who were all more than willing to sacrifice one of their kidneys, but six were unable to donate a kidney, due to health reasons. Only one sister, Leti was considered for my transplant. My husband was a match but after further testing was not allowed to be my donor. We have two daughters, Michelle and Jackie. Jackie was automatically ruled out due to bouts with kidney stones. Michelle was also found to be a good match and was next in line after my sister Leti. By the grace of God and my sister's determination, she worked really hard to meet the transplant teams' qualifications. I was finally going to get my kidney transplant.

On November 4, 2016, our kidney transplant was performed and it was a complete success. My sister and I are both doing well. I am so grateful to my sister for giving me the gift of "life" and a second chance for a normal life. I have had to continue to work hard to protect my new kidney from being rejected, which could cause me to lose my kidney my dear sister gave me. I can't explain the bond I have with my sister who basically saved my life. But I know that none of this would've been possible without God by my side.

I have since retired from my job of 33 years. I miss it but I felt it necessary in order to concentrate on my health. We have since began attending church every Sunday, receive communion on a regular basis, volunteer at our church and local elementary school and also got married by the church, as a symbol of our devotion to God. Yes, it was what was missing in our life, in our marriage and in my recovery.

I will forever be grateful for the lessons I have learned along the way. I would never have known that by experiencing something so difficult would later bring me more peace, more patience, a stronger faith, hope for the future and a heart overflowing with gratitude. – *Idalia Leal*

Reflection: Medical procedures at times can be terrifying and overwhelming. The love, support and prayers from family and friends, can do wonders in easing the pain and anxiety of a loved one during difficult times. – Henry Trevino

My Life Flashed Before Me

Be on your guard. Remain strong in the faith. Be brave. Be loving in everything you do. 1Corinthians 16:13

My partner, paramedic Cliff Aultman, and I had just come in from an emergency call we had made an hour earlier. It was 8 p.m. and we had just sat down to unwind when the emergency radio alerted us to a call coming in. The information we got from the alarm dispatcher was for an unconscious person. We immediately jumped into ambulance and proceeded to the address we had received from fire alarm.

Upon arrival a man who looked quite frazzled greeted us at the door. He escorted us up to a small 2nd story apartment in a very large semi-Victorian home. When we got upstairs, we walked into a windowless, centrally located apartment. The apartment was completely dark. The only lights my partner and I had were the small penlights that we usually used to check pupillary reaction of unconscious persons.

As I started looking through the apartment, I saw a figure laid out on the floor. As my partner and I approached the figure, I noticed that the person was wearing camouflage pants, no shoes and no shirt. He lay face down and motionless. As I slowly approached him, I noticed multiple pill containers and bottles of liquor on the floor; all empty.

Next to the person on the floor was a toppled orange-colored plastic tumbler. In the tumbler were what seemed to be semi-disintegrated capsules. It looked as if this person had put a bunch of pills in the glass, filled it with liquor and drank the contents. Having gone through this scenario many times before, we assumed that it was an apparent overdose. I slowly approached the person on the floor while still just using my small pen light.

I started to check for a pulse on his wrist. As I was reaching down to check for a pulse, I saw something between his fingers. For some reason, as I was checking for his wrist something sinister caught my eye. As I looked closer, I came eye to eye with an old style *'pineapple'* hand grenade.

The man on the floor had placed the hand grenade in his left hand. He had put his right-hand finger through the pin, (the ring); then laid face down on his left forearm. He placed one hand over the other. We later learned that it was a tactic that he apparently learned in Vietnam many, many years ago; in this position, when a person would turn him over, the pin would come out and the grenade would explode; hence he booby-trapped himself.

It was a miracle that I happened to see it and I'm glad that I understood what it was. I dropped my penlight and with both my hands I grabbed his two hands and clasped them together as tight as I could. At this point I could do nothing more but to hold his hands together and all the while enveloping my hands around the grenade. I yelled out to my partner who was standing next to me; *"Hey this so-and-so is holding a hand grenade and is ready to pull the pin!"* While all this was going on the man's mother, who had followed us upstairs, said, *"Oh that must be the one he had hanging on the wall."*

The patient eventually became semiconscious and started to move around. He never said a word, but I do remember that he was very strong. He struggled to get up and managed to shake me around like a rag doll. While all this was going on, I never let go of his hands. What followed was very violent. His brother came into the room to help us subdue him. The violent ruckus stopped only after his brother pulled his legs out from under him. We both fell to the floor with me on top. After we fell. I remember seeing the refrigerator lying on its side, the table broken in two and felt severe pain on my face.

My partner had already called for police backup. The patient was barely breathing but I refused to let go of his hands. My partner did the best he could to provide care for the patient, but it was almost impossible due to the position we were in while lying on the floor.

When the police officer arrived, I realized that he had no backup. The officer peeked around the door and asked, *"Where's the grenade?"* My partner told him that I had it controlled in my two-handed grasp. The police officer very slowly moved my fingers off of the patient's hands and was able to slowly pull his finger from the ring on the pin in the grenade. The police officer took the grenade and left the room.

By this time another paramedic crew arrived and started working on the now limp and unconscious patient. My partner and I followed the other E.M.S. crew that was transporting the patient to BAMC hospital. The patient was pronounced dead soon after arrival at BAMC hospital. The cause of death was an extreme overdose on Elavil.

I was sitting in the emergency room with an ice pack against my face while trying to make sense of what had just happened. A hospital doctor approached me and gently lifted the ice pack from my swollen and bruised face. He looked at my broken tooth and then yanked a clump of hair entangled in another tooth. That's when I said, *"I must have been screaming."* He looked at me and smiled. He said, *"Yes, you are indeed a very lucky man."*

Two weeks after the incident I was sought out by a San Antonio Police Department Bomb Squad member. He told me that they had defused and exploded the grenade. He also told me that because of the grenade's age the fuse had deteriorated to about 1 second from activating the grenade. The officer described the explosion as, *"A big boom."*

I've relived that emergency call many times. I've often thought; what if we had not been there, what if he had pulled the pin before we got there, what if I had not noticed or seen the grenade, what if that refrigerator had fallen on top of me, what if, what if? In my mind there has never been an end to the 'what ifs.'

During my long career as a firefighter/paramedic I have relived many close calls. My job quickly convinced me that prayer was very necessary. There were a lot of incidents where I called for God's help. The incident with the grenade is the one that really brought me to the point that I saw the face of God. At that moment I knew that I needed more help. I called on the Virgin de Guadalupe, (*Guadalupana*), the mother of God. I knew that God's Mother would make him understand that we really needed His help. The fact that we are still alive is proof that God and His Mother were with us the whole time on that emergency call. – *Richard Flores Ozuna*

Reflections: A brave and giving person is someone who is willing to give his or her life for something bigger than himself. When a person is willing to give up his life to save another, he is giving up his most valued possession. In the eyes of God, it is the most noble and honorable act that a human being can perform. – Henry Trevino

My Life's Odyssey

Create in me a clean heart, O God, and put a new and right spirit within me. – Psalm 51:10

As an aircraft mechanic, I work overseas in 90-day rotations. During the last rotation, before I left, my wife said, *"Oh by the way, can you please write a short story for my book project that I'm working on."*

During the long flight overseas, I found myself thinking about what my wife had asked of me. I was feeling very emotional about leaving this time as I had a gut feeling that my mom was going to pass away while I was overseas. She was not doing well as her health had been deteriorating. The last time I visited which was right before I left, the look in her eyes probably mirrored mine and we both knew it would be the last time we'd see each other. I believe my story began with that thought.

Reflecting on my life, I think about the many things I have done, my accomplishments, my family, things I would do differently, regrets, things I still want to do, my spiritual life and all the people I love who have passed away.

It was not long after arriving when I got the call that my mom had passed away. In my mind I had been preparing for what I thought was going to happen, so I wasn't shocked, yet it was my heart that was not prepared. My siblings suggested that we would have her memorial services once I got back. In a way I was relieved, yet I knew it would be hard for me to grieve my way through this not being close to my family and loved ones.

I lost my sister Diane, my brother Bob, my father and now my mother. I know that it isn't possible to have our family members around forever in this world, as much as I wish we could. I miss them all so much and sometimes it pains me so much that it hurts every part of my soul. The only thing that brings me some comfort is the belief that I will reunite with them again one day.

My parents were some of the hardest working people I ever knew. Their love for their children is what motivated them to give us everything we wanted or needed, within reason. Growing up we never had a lot of money, but we had things money couldn't buy; love, generosity, compassion, lots of laughter and God.

I wish that I had known then what I know now. I'm sure my parents knew how much I loved them, but in my younger years, I sometimes feel like I didn't show them enough, and on top of that I got in trouble a lot, which made it harder for my parents to raise me.

I joined the U.S. Army when I was seventeen, unlike what my parents wanted me to do, which was to stay in school. I thought I knew everything, until I was in basic training. The first chance I was able to call home, I realized how young I really was. The minute I heard my mom's voice, I broke down and cried like a baby, I missed her so much.

Then my dad, my hero and a Marine got on the phone and said, *"Hang in there, son, one day you will become a man."* I always knew that I wanted to be a good man, just like him. He was a tough and dedicated Marine; in my younger years he thought that if he swatted me on the butt, he would hurt me, so my mom was the disciplinary one in the house. My mom would always apologize for all the spankings she gave me when I was a child every single time I came home on leave. I responded, *"Mom, you know I deserved every spanking that I received."* We both knew part of who I had become, was thanks to her.

I married at a very early age while in the military, and was blessed to have my daughter, Stephanie. Although one of my regrets was that I didn't graduate from college, I will say that I absolutely loved being in the military. I served for 10 years in the Army, worked and lived in places all over the world. I have had the opportunity to fly over many different places with a view from a helicopter. Wherever the aircraft went, I would go and it was the best feeling in the world

Once while stationed in Germany, we would respond with alerts, which meant mock wartime scenarios. At times it was fun and exciting and other times it could be very stressful depending on how big the chances were of it actually being the real thing. As soon as we would get the call, within the hour we had to start packing up the aircraft and our company trucks with equipment so we could mobilize, head out and meet the enemy anywhere in the world where needed.

During the time when Iran had taken hostages at the American Embassy, the alerts became much more frequent. It had become more dangerous and that is when I decided to send my wife and daughter back to the states until things cooled down. There were many Middle Eastern people living in Germany at the time and were constantly protesting in the streets of Frankfurt.

The constant threats to attack the military headquarters kept us flying close by with at least 10 other helicopters prepared to land on the roof of the building with our M60 machine guns locked and loaded and prepared to rescue all personnel that worked there.

Thank God that nothing like that happened and we were able to stand down for a few days, although then we got a call ordering us to fly our aircraft over to Rein-Main Air Base, load our aircraft on C5 aircraft and get ready to move out. We flew for quite a few hours and when we landed, to our surprise, we were in a desert in Saudi Arabia. I turned to the guys next to me and said, *"Well boys, I think it's time to fight!"* Turns out we got fuel, stayed on the ground for a while and before we knew it, we were off again, landed in Germany and proceeded to take our own aircraft and return to our base.

It wasn't until after we arrived back to our base that we found out about the failed attempt to rescue the hostages in Iran happened in the desert and we lost some men that day. I can't really tell you what happened but maybe they used us as a decoy so the Iranians would think that the mission was coming from Germany. I have realized how much I trusted God during those times of uncertainty.

Several years later, my wife gave me "the talk," of how we had just grown apart, so we ended up divorcing. Many years have passed since then and other relationships have come and gone, but honestly, my only regret is time that I lost with my family. Leaving home at such an early age to join the military, I traveled the world, which I enjoyed but I was never physically close to my hometown and feel in a way that I let my parents down in ways that are hard to explain.

When I tried to make up for lost time, they were in their older years and weren't able to get around as much. I only hope that during our last visits, they didn't see the sadness in my eyes; that if eyes could speak, they would say, *"I'm sorry I wasn't around as much as I wanted. If only we had more time, I would make things better."* Then again, maybe it's my imagination, but either way, I have let it go and know now that my parents couldn't be happier than where they are now.

Life in the military came with many rewards though. I am proud for having served my country. Many times, I was in life and death situations, I've seen things I would've rather not seen, but I grew up, learned many lessons, traveled the world and survived all the dangers involved in war zones.

God continues to save me and bless me. I have since remarried to someone very special. My wife, Letty, has two children and we have two beautiful grandchildren so far. I have never been happier being a "gramps". What happened? I've been blessed. Now I'm on to our next adventure, our golden years and our grandkids. – *Ernest Ramirez*

Reflection: If cry you must, then cry for a while. Now remember your loved ones without tears in your eyes. Remember the smiles and the memories of ones so dear. Rejoice and thank God that he allowed these wonderful souls to cross our path, gladden our hearts and bring us so much joy. – Henry Trevino

My Mother

Start children off on the right path. And even when they are old, they will not turn away from it. Proverbs 22:6

My mother had a long and beautiful life; she had a brief and beautiful death. At the young age of 62, my mother suffered a massive stoke. When she passed away, she was 87 years old. Even though her way of life had changed, it never changed the quality of it. The significance of that is that my mom never stopped living. She accepted her disability and loss of speech with such courage, grace and strength.

Mom was a devout Catholic and had a heart for God. She was a gentle soul, who lit up a room with her laughter. Her beautiful face never seemed to age; probably because she never participated in any drama, much less cause any. She always seemed to just go with the flow, and never complained about anything. No matter where she was at any given moment, she made it perfectly clear that she was good, and all was well.

The second half of my life was after she had her stroke. My son Christopher was only two years old. She was a consistent figure in all of her grandchildren's life and even several great grandchildren. She inspired all of us to never give up just by the way she lived her life.

My siblings and I are so grateful that we were blessed to have our mother for as long as we did. She had her own special and unique relationship with all of her children. She loved everyone unconditionally. It brings us much comfort knowing that she is now with our dad. She loved my dad with her whole heart. She would put her hand on her heart, and I would ask her, *"You miss Daddy"* and she would nod yes; if her eyes could talk, she would be saying, *"I miss him, but I will continue to wait patiently for him to come for me."*

How blessed we feel that her grandchildren and some of her great grandchildren got to know her before she passed. She offered a piece of her heart without asking for anything in return. She never wanted to be a burden to anyone, loved being with her family but also liked her space. Her favorite show of all time was *The Price Is Right;* she looked so forward to that show and loved to see people winning.

After our dad passed away, for the next 7 years she found her place in each of our homes. It was a pleasure to care for her. She brought joy wherever she went. She liked being as independent as possible and help whenever she could. It was known by all of us that wherever she was, she liked to help us with certain things. At my house she was the one that always closed the blinds when the sun went down; she made sure the doors were locked at night; she would let me know if the trash cans needed to go out or come in, notified me of the mailman at the curb and reminded me to feed the dogs. Since she visited and stayed with all her children, she had her own unique duties that she liked to be in charge of.

The fact that my daughter Emily was the youngest of her grandchildren, she probably spent the most time with her. She would come into the house and say in her old cheerleader voice; *"Ok Wela," come on let's go somewhere. It's a beautiful day to get out and get some fresh air. I want you to go with me to HEB and then we can go to sonic and have a treat."* Emily never let her Wela's disability get in the way of taking her anywhere. She was always willing to go the extra mile so that Wela could get out and enjoy herself.

We all knew her schedule like the back of our hand. Even Maci my 3-year-old grandbaby, knew when I said it was 8:30... she would say, *"Its wine time for Wela."* She would get so much joy by serving her Wela. After taking her glass of wine, she already knew the routine. She would hand me her eye drops, and then she would hand me her face cream. At 3 years old, my little Maci knew exactly what my mom needed. The love in my mother's eyes when she would see Maci doing things for her and seeing the joy in Maci's eyes knowing that she enjoyed helping her, it was hard to tell who was the happier of the two. My mother's love for all children was so genuine and real.

My dad used to joke with her and say, *"For not talking, you sure do talk a lot."* We knew exactly what he meant. There were many times when my siblings and I would laugh and say, *"We can't trust you."* If one or two of us would get together perhaps talking about something we didn't want anyone to know and later come to find out she managed to spill the beans. Most of the time, we had no idea how she was even able to communicate such stories without being able to talk. We would then question my mom and jokingly tell her she could just not keep a secret and we were not going to talk in front of her anymore because she talked too much. She would just laugh about it because it was so funny; the same laugh that everyone that had ever been around her knew.

In the last hours of her life when she was given her last rites, she knew what was happening and she was ready to make the transition. My mother was never afraid of dying. All she ever wanted was to live her life according to God's Will. How grateful we were to have our parish priest, Father Martin coming to our aid so quickly and the beautiful way he prayed over our mom.

God arranged the beautiful and gentle way in which she made that transition into her heavenly home. She passed away from a very loving and peaceful environment. We decorated her room with fresh flowers, played beautiful music, placed pictures of my dad around her and the infamous diffuser my sister takes everywhere she goes, was in her room, filled with a subtle scent of lavender oil.

When the time came, my niece, Melissa, described it best, finding the beauty in her passing was easy; her 5 loving daughters surrounded her. As they sang her favorite song, she squinted, almost as if the "light" was so bright. She took her last breath and her angels echoed and answered our imploring voices. Gifted with God's grace, her beautiful soul was then at peace. What a blessing to have been able to be by her side, holding her hand as she made that transition. As we allowed her to leave us, we felt safe knowing that she was welcomed and greeted by loved ones at the gates of heaven. I must say that I am sure our dad was extremely proud that we kept our promise to him that we would take care of our mother, until the end of her life here.

There is absolutely no doubt in our minds, that not only is our mother now talking and walking, but she is now dancing, singing and celebrating in the presence of God the Father and with all her loved ones that have gone before her.

As a family we wanted to dress my mom in white for her funeral, because to us she was, and always would be our angel. We her children chose to wear white also, not because we are perfect little angels but because we loved her so much. She was as perfect as one can get, and as her children we now strive to be more like her. She set an example for everyone. To always love God, have faith in him, trust him, always be grateful, and live your life to the fullest. Also, to forgive any wrongdoings, make your mark in the world by praying, and asking God to reveal what His purpose is for your life.

She will be missed, and we will at times cry and feel lonely here without her, but she was so big in our hearts that her love for us and our love for her will be enough to continue to inspire us and make a difference in how we live our lives. Although I will never be able to live up to my mother's ways, she will still have inspired me to be more than I ever thought I could be.

Her favorite prayer, and song still gives me chills every time I hear it. It was her wish to sing it at her funeral for as long as we can all remember. My siblings and I believe it is the way she tried to live her life. And a beautiful example of how we should try to live ours.

The Prayer of St Francis

Lord, make me an instrument of your peace,
Where there is hatred, let me sow love.
Where there is injury, pardon.
Where there is doubt, faith.
Where there is despair, hope.
Where there is darkness, light.
Where there is sadness, joy.

O Divine Master,
Grant that I may not so much seek
To be consoled as to console;
To be understood as to understand.
To be loved as to love

For it is in giving that we receive.
It is in pardoning that we are pardoned.
And it is in dying that we are born to eternal life.

– Letty Ramirez

Reflection: The words of St. Francis truly defined what our mother practiced and what she strongly believed. Mothers have a special way of living a life of love, sacrifice, and always knowing how to mend a broken heart. The legacy that mothers leave behind will continue to be the inspiration that her loved ones will continue living. – Henry Trevino

My Sophie

Let all that you do be done in love. 1 Corinthians 16:14

When I was in 8th grade, I asked my mom and my stepdad, Bert for a dog. After about a million "no's" Bert finally agreed and said "yes." I had always wanted a little yorkie, so my mom and I started looking through newspapers and found a breeder close by so we went to visit.

When we walked into her house, this woman had like 20 little yorkies running around the house. She offered me one that was a baby, however, we wanted the one that was smiling and following her around. She was two years old and adorable. The lady said, *"Oh I'm sorry she is my baby, my pet and I'm not even thinking about selling her."*

I'm not sure how it happened, but after a little convincing, the one I wanted, whose name was Sophie, was in the car and we were headed home. I remember her shaking, as she had no idea where she was going. Little did she know she was on the road to the best life ever. I bonded with her immediately, and from then on my love for her continued to grow.

During my junior high and high school, she was in my life on a constant basis, but it wasn't until I moved out on my own to an apartment while in college, when I felt even more of a connection. While attending college fulltime and working part-time, she was my baby; I was totally responsible for her care and wellbeing. I remember times when I would come home and tend to her thinking to myself, *"I can't even imagine not having her."* I loved being her mommy, and I looked forward to coming home to her.

This little 6-pound dog was my baby: I loved her, she loved me and I enjoyed spoiling her. I dressed her up and would take her to work; she became the mascot at Voge, the boutique where I worked. The customers loved her too and she absolutely loved all the attention. You would think she was getting paid just to be so cute. I took my little girl with me practically everywhere I went. She would ride with me in the car, fly with me in the airplane, and at times would be my sidekick when doing photo-shoots for work. She even took graduation pictures with me when I graduated from college.

     It was in October of 2017, I noticed that she had not been eating as much as she normally did and had become a little less active. On the 9th of October, I woke up and my heart dropped; my little Sophie could not walk. I also noticed that she had a lump on the side of her throat. I knew something was wrong, so I decided to take her to the vet.

     After a full checkup and X-rays, they diagnosed her with cancer. The vet proceeded to tell me, *"I think you might want to consider putting her down."* With tears in my eyes, I couldn't find the words to respond to her. To make matters worse, she then said, *"I'm not suggesting weeks or months, but days."* Perhaps it was the way she said it, with no hope whatsoever or no compassion for the way I might react to such news.

     I just wasn't prepared for any of this. Maybe I was somewhat in denial, or just not wanting to accept that she was sick, but I was angry at the doctor for being so insensitive and wanting to take such drastic measures. I decided to leave, and I took her to another vet for a second opinion. The other vet had a much better response. First of all, I was comforted by the fact that she was convinced that she was not in any pain. Her plan was to take baby steps to get her better. They put her on an anti-inflammatory and an antibiotic. Slowly, but surely, she began to improve.

About a month later, she got an ulcer in her eye. I had to take her to a specialist where they confirmed that she was not able to see out of one of her eyes, but that they would do whatever they could to save the other one. I had to take her to the doctor a little more often during that time and had to be very consistent with her medicines and eye drops, even when they were required every 4 hours. I would do anything for my Sophie; she was my best friend, my roommate and my baby, even when it meant waking up every 4 hours in the middle of the night.

It was very difficult for me to see her so frail. On top of being the one person she loved and counted on to take care of her, I had just gone through a terrible breakup. I had to take care of not only her but also myself. We were there for each other and we needed each other at this time in my life.

The only other person who knew how I felt and how much I loved Sophie was my mom. She was also the only person I felt comfortable with to take care of Sophie when I wasn't able to. When she was first diagnosed with cancer, the vet told me that I did have the option of surgery and extensive treatment for Sophie, but it would not guarantee that she would be cured or that she would even survive. On top of that it was going to be very expensive.

Even though I had the money in my savings, and I would have done anything for Sophie, my mom suggested that we pray about it. I didn't think deep in my heart that God would want me to spend all my money towards this expense when all I would need to do is to turn her over into God's care and trust that His will be done.

As soon as mom and I decided that the best thing to do would be to take it a day at a time, she did some research online and purchased some natural drops that had great results for dogs with this condition. We took those drops to Deacon Rich at our church and had him bless them.

God blessed us with 8 more months together. Although she had so many problems at that time, from cancer, to liver disease, to fluid in her lungs, her eye problems, she was looking and acting so much better. She was gaining weight, running around and happy. It was truly a miracle.

That miracle that I witnessed started when I turned the situation over to God. During those eight months, I prayed this prayer: *Dear God, You know how much I love Sophie. If it is your will, please allow her to stay with me a little longer. I want her to be comfortable and happy and in no pain. Help me to relax and enjoy her company, without worrying when I will have to let her go. I ask that you let me know when her time comes and that she will pass in peace. In Jesus name Amen.*

When the time came, it was quickly and peacefully but still difficult for me. I grew and I learned from that experience. And God comforted me during those trying times. I realized how much of a fighter she was. Even when she was sick, she had so much energy and light. She was always happy and lovable. I felt good that I had given her the life she deserved. And most of all I thank God for the love he showed me. Since then, I have witnessed miracles in other areas of my life by simply surrendering everything to God and allowing him to take care of everything in his time according to his will.

The day after Sophie was put down, I went to my mom's house to spend the day swimming with family. Out of nowhere, a beautiful butterfly began flying around us. Of all the people there, it chose to land on my hand. I believe that was my little Sophie. She was reassuring me that she was happy and free. – *Emily Carpenter*

Reflection: Prayer is your call to God. God in his mercy will never turn you away. When you touch the heart of God, miracles will indeed appear. – Henry Trevino

Proclamation Of Love

And over all these good things put on love. Love holds them all together perfectly as if they were one. Colossians- 3:14

My wife and I have shared twice in this life what some people hope to share once in a lifetime. We have both stepped from one beautiful dream into another just as beautiful. Fate brought us together in a way neither of us expected.

Both, my wife and I lost our first loves many years before we met. I lost my wife, Marty, in 1983; Mary Lou, my present wife lost her husband, Roy, in 1991. Our dear companions passed away unexpectedly many years before we ever met. After their deaths we both floundered around not knowing which direction to follow. We both made many friends during the times we were alone. The friends that we made along the way never seemed to stick around for any length of time. We both continued our lonely travel, promising ourselves that we would never get close to another person again.

Our coming together was surprising and unexpected. It grew from a simple meeting, to a relationship, and eventually a marriage. How it happened; some dear friends insisted that I should meet their friend, Mary Lou. We both refused their invitation to meet many times. Eventually, with their constant insistence we decided to meet. After our initial meeting we became inseparable friends. We saw each other every day, enjoyed our friends and celebrated our good fortunate. We eventually got married and lived a great life together for 22 years.

Unfortunately, Mary Lou passed away unexpectedly in 2014. As it was with my first wife, Marty, the day the ambulance took them to the hospital was the last time I saw them alive. I did not even get to say goodbye to them. What I have now is the memories of two great women.

I decided to write this story to describe my first love from the past and the love that I shared with Mary Lou in what I considered my second life. Likewise, Mary Lou lived with the memories of her first love, however, she accepted my love and she willingly gave me her love.

Webster defines Love as "the feeling experienced when one is strongly attached or deeply devoted to another." In my humble opinion I think it is the kind of feeling, (love), that everyone can experience. There are, however, many kinds of love; there is love for your parents, love for your children, love for your friends and love for life itself. However, the love between husband and wife is different; it runs deep, it is constant; it is in a perpetual state of growth and not wasting in stagnation. Love between a husband and wife is personal, it is exciting, it is not public and most important, it is to be shared only by a husband and wife.

When it comes to love, we have truly lived it. We have both experienced it in the past and now together we continue in our own private way to share the love that can be shared only by a husband and wife. A love that did not replace our first dream, but a love built on a new foundation. Our love has been built and nurtured by two people that dared to dream. The love we have is seen only by two people as they gaze into the eyes of the other. Our love is reserved for only two people; it is a love that only my wife and I know is only ours.

It is not important that the love of a husband and wife must be shown to prove its existence; you don't have to hold hands to prove its closeness; you don't have to kiss in public to prove its intensity; you don't have to be together 100 percent of the time to prove its loyalty. What is important is that only the two people know it's there and that it's there only to be shared with each other.

Some people are very good at showing love. Some people are utter failures. I guess I fall into the latter category. Again, in my humble opinion, I feel that just knowing that you are loved by someone should be enough. How does the saying go, "actions speak louder than words?" You don't say, *"I love you,"* fifteen times a day. After a while the words become mundane and overused. A person may only say it once a week, but that one time is welcomed and appreciated much more than hearing it many times each day.

You quietly show your love by being home every night. You help with the dishes and the laundry. If something breaks you fix it. If there is a party, you go together. You enjoy your children, your grandchildren and your friends. You enjoy each other's jokes even if they're not funny.

The important thing is that you just do things together, and most importantly you enjoy each other's company. Those are the little things that count and give value to the true meaning of love. The small everyday experiences that are shared by a husband and wife are what solidify a union, slowly intensifying the love for each other. I have come to believe that a very thin line separates the ones who think they are in love and desperately try to show it and the ones who don't feel the need to show it because in their hearts they truly feel love. A husband and wife walk as one, finding it unnecessary to publicly proclaim their love for each other.

Each group can live in their own world with their own beliefs, viewpoints, and philosophies. One group can feel that their love is a very beautiful and splendid thing that must be shouted from the highest peaks. The other group will continue to quietly live their lives knowing their love for each other is truly theirs and not to be shared.

When it comes to true love only the husband and wife know it's their special love; there to be shared privately between themselves. I am grateful to God that he gave me the opportunity to marry two wonderful women. I will die knowing in my heart that my wives knew that I loved them dearly.

In closing, I leave you with the words of a song that I heard many years ago that gave meaning to the word, "love." The words were; *"Love is a many-splendored thing; I say no moon in the sky ever lent such a glow."* That beautiful glow is the eyes of a woman in love. That is as close as anyone can come to the description of love. – *Henry Trevino*

Reflections: Love is hidden in your inner self. It will not mature and blossom until it is given away. It is like a seed; unless it is planted it will not germinate and grow to a beautiful flower. Do not withhold your love. One should give it generously so that it can sprout and become a really beautiful flower in another person's heart. Giving your love is the ultimate gift that will last forever.
–*Henry Trevino*

Reality Check

But those who trust in the LORD will receive new strength. They will fly as high as eagles. They will run and not get tired. They will walk and not grow weak. Isaiah – 40:31

July 26, 2016 was the day that changed my reality. Prior to this day, my reality was one of contentment and happiness with my family and myself. Although I had a few health issues, which weren't unusual for a 67-year-old, I felt great and was a very active person. So, I wasn't prepared when I received a call from my physician. I was told that they had discovered a mass on the upper lobe on my right lung and that it could be cancer. That same day my pulmonologist confirmed that indeed the mass appeared to be cancer. A week later a biopsy revealed that I had non-small cell lung cancer.

Both my pulmonologist and oncologist felt that I could be cured but would have to put my life on hold for about six months while I underwent radiation, chemo and surgery. The really scary part was that the surgery would involve removing my right upper lobe, a portion of 3 ribs and part of my chest wall, which then would have to be reconstructed.

Flashback; six months prior to that cancer diagnosis, I started experiencing a slight pain in my right shoulder blade. At first, I wrote it off as just a new pain like others I had experienced that would go away; just a normal ache or pain that went with getting older. As weeks went by the pain worsened, so my wife, Elsa, insisted I visit our family doctor, which I did. Based on my description of the pain in my back he suspected that it was associated with my cervical spine. He sent me to physical therapy, which really helped, and the pain all but went away. I was relieved, at least for a while. Unfortunately, after a couple of weeks the pain returned with a vengeance.

In my heart of hearts, I had always felt that the pain was something far more serious than I wanted to believe. In hindsight, I probably downplayed the severity of my pain both with my doctors and myself. Had the pain not become unbearable I may never have gone for further tests. Additional tests ultimately revealed that indeed I did have something far more serious than pain caused by the normal aches and pains of an aging cervical spine.

I truly believe that most people go through a denial of sorts when it comes to having an undiagnosed pain, rationalizing that it's nothing serious to worry about. I think this is especially true of us men. Who knows, had I taken my symptoms more seriously sooner, perhaps I could have avoided surgery or at the least less serious surgery without the removal of my ribs. It turned out that the extreme pain was caused by the tumor pressing nerves against my ribs and was actually eroding three of my ribs.

That first night after the devastating diagnosis of stage II cancer I cried like a baby out of self-pity, fear and despair. Although my doctors thought I would survive and even had a chance to be cured, I felt totally alone and scared to death. My wife was an angel and rock of strength in comforting me that first night. I can't say enough about my sweet wife and the constant care and love she gave me and of course still does. Without her, I am certain I wouldn't have prevailed as I have. That same night I turned to God in prayer asking for the strength and courage to see me through this crisis and to ultimately heal and cure me of this horrible disease. God answered by giving me the strength, courage and hope to kick the heck out of cancer and win my battle.

Of course, I shared my diagnosis with family members and friends and although I shouldn't have been surprised, I learned that I was on countless prayer lists even in churches outside of San Antonio and Texas. In fact, there wasn't a day that went by that I didn't receive an email, text or card in the mail that buoyed my spirits.

During my radiation treatments, I met a couple, Dan and Diane. Diane was undergoing radiation from her original breast cancer, which had metastasized, to her leg and even other parts of her body. She had survived and endured her illness from this insidious disease for 10 years, yet there she was with such a radiant smile and positive disposition that I couldn't help but feel great hope for my own survival.

I have no doubt that God placed her in that radiation treatment center on that very day to be an inspiration for me. Diane had the same daily radiation treatment schedule as I did so it didn't take long before Diane and Dan felt like family. One day Dan invited me to a men's group at his church. I took him up on the invite and without going into detail, I can tell you that it had a profound positive effect on my prayer life and gave me even more hope and courage to conquer my disease. Dan also invited me to our local McDonalds where he and two of his friends, Bert and Doug, met nearly every morning and discussed the latest news and also prayed and read Bible scriptures.

These three special friends and their prayers played a major role in my cancer battle. I still meet with these gentlemen daily. To my amazement, people that we don't even know, some of which are suffering from cancer, often visit our table in need of a smile and a prayer. In the meantime, I learned that a dear friend, Lynda Jo from my high school days was diagnosed with stage 4 brain cancer. Although I hadn't seen Lynda Jo in years, we quickly became bonded for our common purpose of beating cancer. Once again, I believe that God had placed someone in my life for the purpose of helping me fight my disease.

This was also an opportunity for me to help someone who was suffering worse than I was. It was a reminder from God that there are others that are suffering and need someone to give them courage. So, this is exactly what I tried to do with Lynda Jo. I believe in my own way that I was able to help her through my daily prayers and the encouragement I continued to give her.

On December 27, 2016, five months after my diagnosis I completed my last chemo treatment. By the way, chemo really SUCKS. I can't begin to describe how sick it made me. Nonetheless, on January 18, I had my first post treatment CT scan and a week later learned that I was cancer free. While I will need to have periodic CT scans for years to come, I have the faith that only our Lord can provide that I will be pronounced cured 5 years from now. I am regaining my strength and energy and am beginning to enjoy my life once again *ONE DAY AT A TIME.*

I look out my window today and see beautiful blue skies and a bright sunny day just begging me to go out and live life to the fullest and not worry about tomorrow. So that's exactly what I did! – Dale R. Hart

Reflection: Life as we know it would cease to exist without hope. Every facet of life depends on hope. Hope is the God given gift that nourishes our beings, gives us courage, a meaning to our existence, and expectation of a future. – Henry Trevino

The Beginning of a Long Career

The Lord will command his angels to take good care of you.
Psalm 91:11

After four years of sacrifice, study and doing without, I officially became a college graduate. I was ready to start making the big money everyone talked about. I had a wife and three children to support. But as I entered the job market, I soon came to the realization that jobs were not very plentiful. An uncle of mine, fire engineer Andrew San Miguel, suggested I look into employment with the San Antonio Fire Department. I talked it over with my wife and we both decided that perhaps this job could help us, at least until something better came along. I took the Fire Department test and was placed on the eligibility list.

After taking my medical, physical and psychological exams I proceeded with the last part of the recruitment process, which was going before a screening board. I was eventually hired and ordered to report for duty on October 1, 1961. This is the day when I first stepped into the firehouse. I was instructed to report to station #3. Unbeknownst to me, this was one of the busiest stations in the department. This station, almost being in the center of town, responded to most of the regular alarms sounded.

I can remember everything that occurred on that date; from the moment I awoke in the morning, said goodbye to my wife and three children, and returning home after my first day on the job. When I reported to the officer on duty, his first words were, *"I don't know why they sent you here. I don't need anybody."* The officer made a few calls and confirmed that I was indeed assigned to this particular station.

The officer asked one of the firefighters going off duty to lend me a fire-fighting coat. They scrounged around and found an old helmet that I could use. The officer took me to the joker stand, (a narrow table where the radio and speaker were located), and said; *"See that box, it's a radio. When you hear 3 beeps or the number 3 sounded, get on the pumper and hold on."*

One hour and thirty minutes after I stepped into the fire station, we received our first alarm. It was a call for a bomb ready to explode. It turned out to be a false alarm. The second regular alarm sounded thirty minutes after we had gotten back to the fire station. It was a call for a house on fire. We could see fire and smoke from blocks away. The house was in full bloom and the houses on either side were catching on fire.

Until this time the biggest fire I had ever seen was inside of a bar-b-que pit. While we were fighting the fire, we could hear loud popping noises. We thought the pops were from exploding firecrackers. We later learned that they were boxes of shotgun and rifle shells. This was about the time I started to have second thoughts about being a firefighter.

Our third regular alarm came in at 3 a.m. The radio instructed the responding fire fighters that it was an explosion. My company, #3, was the first one on the scene. The explosion had been so violent that the roof and the walls were blown across the street. I witnessed my first burn death at this fire. All this happened on my first shift, even before I started training to become a firefighter.

When we got back to the station an old district chief who was also stationed there noticed that I was not very happy. He came over to talk to me trying to make me feel better. I don't remember the conversation; however, I never forgot his last words; *"Trevino, it's not always this bad. Stick with it. It's going to get better. We'll be getting newer and better equipment. Stay with it and look to the future, the best is yet to come."*

During my long career I was taken to the hospital no less than ten times with some minor injuries and injuries that were serious. Burns, cuts, smoke and chemical inhalation were some of the injuries that were part of the job. I witnessed happy, sad and tragic endings. The alarms that we responded to were generally for, fires, wrecks, drownings, shootings, explosions, collapsed buildings, sick persons, heart attacks, etc. 99% of our calls resulted in some one losing their house or other valuable property. In addition to the loss of property came the terrible injuries and many times death – all of which the survivors had to contend with.

I have been retired for 24 years and I still remember tragic events that I responded to; injured families, death of children in automobile wrecks and badly burned adults and children. Those visions don't go away, they surface every once in a while, and shake you into the present reality.

The Fire Department eventually went from a 15-company baby to a 44-station giant. I experienced the evolution of arson, fire prevention and vehicle repair shops. I witnessed the creation of Haz-Mat, (hazardous materials), rescue units, boats for flood rescue, drowning recovery, and the birth of E.M.S. (emergency medical services), with its highly trained paramedics came into being.

Who in 1961 would have dreamed of the Hurst tool, better known as *the jaws of life*? The Hurst tool was capable of dissecting a car in minutes, cutting or wedging the strongest steel. Back then we were not issued gloves or facemasks. We never used the breathing apparatus because they usually never worked. If you wanted gloves or a flashlight you had to buy them at your expense. Radios to communicate with other units or for rescue of trapped fire fighters were nonexistent; 90% of today's tools were not available in 1961.

A lot has changed since 1961, but the one thing about that year that makes it so special to me is that job eventually became a profession. Now, 35 years later, I realize it was my life, my true career. Looking back, I cannot imagine going through life not being a firefighter. I thank God that he gave me the health, physical and emotional strength and the privilege to work with, and for my fellow man

I continue to this day to live my life with purpose. I have always tried to do my best in all areas of my life, never settling for second best. Many times, I didn't succeed, but I knew I had given it my best shot. I have coined an adage that I have lived with all my life; "never do less today than you did yesterday." Always add a few steps to your run, read an extra page, say an extra thank you, or show an extra act of kindness.

The lasting words of my career that are still etched in my heart are the words from that old District Chief; *"Look to the future, for the best is yet to come." – Henry Trevino*

Reflections: Looking back on all those years makes me smile with gratitude. I had a passion, a desire, a craving to do the best that I could do. The things you will do for your fellow man in this life will be your treasure and legacy by which your family and friends will remember you. – Henry Trevino

The Circle of Life

Children are a gift from the Lord. They are a reward from him. Children who are born to people when they are young are like arrows in the hands of a soldier. Blessed are those who have many children. They won't be put to shame when they go up against their enemies in court. Psalm 127:3-5

My husband, Lloyd and I have been together for over 13 years. We had big plans early on in our relationship. We enjoyed traveling, had an active social life and delighted in the fact that we could be spontaneous. We absolutely loved the freedom to do what we wanted, when we wanted. We were mom and dad only to our dogs, and that is just the way we wanted it. We had decided even before we got married, that we wouldn't have children. We were so set on it; all we wanted, was to be awesome partners in a marriage, determined to be "the fun" aunt and uncle to our nieces and nephews and just live our lives as is ... forever.

Lloyd's mother comes from a large and extremely close family. We have always enjoyed spending time with our families. Whether it was traveling together, sharing Holidays, dinners, BBQ or just visiting, we were making memories. My husband was especially close to his grandfather, his mom's father. When his grandfathers' health became an issue, he began struggling with his oxygen levels and needed to use an oxygen tank on a regular basis. He also had a few bad falls which set him back to the point of not wanting to eat which caused him to become very weak.

When we received the phone call that the end was near, my husband and I rushed to his grandparent's house so he could be with his parents, aunts, uncles and cousins. He wanted a chance to say his final goodbyes to his grandfather. I didn't know at the time that his death would change our lives forever.

All I wanted during this time was to be there for my husband who was having a very difficult time with the death of his grandfather. One night, I suggested that we go out for dinner, just the two of us, and try to get our minds off everything, at least for a while.

During the middle of our dinner, out of the blue, my husband said, *"I think we should have a baby."* I didn't know what to say at first, but I asked him, *"What changed your mind?"* His response made me tear up even to this day. *"I loved my grandfather so much and standing next to all my aunts and uncles that day he passed away, I realized just how much he meant to his children."*

He wanted that; the unconditional love of a family. I had never been adamantly against having kids, I just figured if my husband wanted them someday I would too. After seeing his reasoning and change of heart, I couldn't help but feel the same way he did. It was the best decision we ever made. Today we are blessed with two children. We have a daughter, Sloane who is 5 years old and a son, Lane who is almost a year old. Of course, it is a lot of work to be parents, but we cannot imagine our lives without them. They are our biggest achievements.

We miss our grandfather every single day, but we will always cherish the memories we made, and all the lessons he taught us. Thinking of him sometimes brings a tear to our eyes, yet always followed by a smile, as his death revealed to us the unconditional love and the joy it brings to have children of our own. We are so grateful and blessed to have such a wonderful family. – *Marissa Alexander*

Reflection: The greatest gift bestowed on us by God is our children. The greatest gifts parents can give to their children are roots and wings. They will one day also thank you for the lessons you taught them and the many memories they will forever cherish.
– Henry Trevino

The Importance of Forgiveness

No temptation has overtaken you except what is common to mankind. And God is faithful; he will not let you be tempted beyond what you can bear. But when you are tempted, he will also provide a way out so that you can endure it. Corinthians 10:13

I grew up in a home with loving parents and God in and out of my life. We would go to church every now and then and on holidays so I would say faith was a part of my upbringing, but it wouldn't be until later in life that I truly found my faith and love for God.

I remember the incident that radically changed my life like it was yesterday. My brother and I were getting ready for bed when my parents called us in the living room and began to explain to us that we were going to have a visitor. At that time, I was so young; I didn't know exactly why he was coming or how long he was going to stay. I was so excited because my older brother was my best friend and now, I was going to have two best friends. My parents explained that Michael would begin coming quite frequently.

My mom had been working really hard to set up new bunk beds so that we would all have a place to sleep when he came over. When he arrived, he was very quiet, but we understood, as this was new for all of us. My mom did a great job to help him feel comfortable as part of our family. Things went smoothly and we began to look forward to his future visits.

All was well, until that one night that changed everything. We were all sleeping. I was awakened late in the night by a sound of someone whispering my name ... it was Michael. I asked him what he was doing, and he asked me if I wanted to play a game? Of course, I wanted to play a game, so I eagerly said *"Yes,"* just like any child would. What happened next was something I will never forget. The very thing our parents pray that will never happen to our children happened to me; Michael molested me.

At the time, I had no idea what had happened to me, but it felt wrong. When it was over, he told me that if I ever told anyone, especially my parents, that they would be mad at me. I was scared and didn't want that to happen. For the next 18 years, it would be a secret, that later turned into anger and sadness. It wasn't until a few years later, that I realized what happened. And I began to question why God would allow this terrible thing to happen to me; I was just an innocent little girl.

In the midst of my anger and sadness, I began to recall other things that seemed to have affected me as a child. When I was in 8th grade, my dad decided to leave my mom. I remember asking God, *"How could you put my family and I through this?" "What did I do to deserve this? My mom didn't deserve this either."* I knew I couldn't let my mom see me sad. She had done so well at being strong and positive through it all. Deep down I knew she was sad, but she held it all together and she tried to never let us see her cry.

After my dad moved out, he began to see another woman. I grew even more sad and angry with everyone, especially God. I was angry with God for ripping my family apart. I remember one day after coming home from school, I overheard my mom crying loudly in her room. My heart hurt and at that moment, I tried reasoning with God. I asked him to please put my family back together and I would never question him again.

I promised my God and Creator that I would always love him, and I would do whatever he wanted me to do; however that was not how things worked out. I began to act out and do things out of anger and heartache. It led me to drinking in the 8th grade, which, little did I know, would end up being my worst enemy the next few years.

In high school, I tried to be as happy as possible. I was involved with school activities that took up most of my time, but my relationship with my parents became distant and my relationship with God no longer existed. I began to party every weekend and getting in trouble constantly. I began lying to my parents about where I was or what I was doing.

At the end of my junior year, I started dating Andrew, a guy I went to middle school with. Our relationship started out good, but it later turned into a traumatic, emotional, and abusive three-year relationship. My friends tried to convince me to leave him; they witnessed how bad things had gotten and how my other relationships, especially with my family were strained. I had distanced myself from all my family members.

There was a point in time when I was so sad, that I truly believed my family and my friends would be better off without me. Sometimes, I would ask myself, *"Why can't I just leave and walk away? It seemed so simple, right?"* I remember during those times, I would randomly pray to God and ask him to give me the strength I needed to walk away. But the strength never came, and the abuse went on.

When I started college, the drinking and partying only got worse. The drinking made me numb to the sadness and pain I had gone through throughout the years. I got multiple MIP's, noise violations, and probably could have died multiple times from alcohol poisoning.

One spring day, the mental and emotional abuse coming from my boyfriend finally turned physical. We had been drinking at the pool at his apartment all day and had just gotten home. I can never remember exactly what I said or did to cause him to snap, it all happened so quickly. I do remember there was yelling, and things were thrown and broken, and before I knew it, there was a hand across my face. I fell back on the bed and could taste the blood in my mouth from my lip, which was busted open.

I was in shock and scared for my life. As he frantically began apologizing, I slowly gathered my things to leave. When I left that day, I never went back. I got in my car; and I began to pray, *"Lord, if you are listening, I get it now, please protect me and help me through this."* I drove home in silence. Finally, God had given me the strength I needed to leave that day, but I was still not happy with God. I still wanted to know why God would allow these terrible things to happen to me. I never got an answer, which helped deplete all the faith I had left.

In April of 2016, I was invited to go on an ACTS Retreat for women. I really didn't want to go, but my friend insisted and convinced me to go. I figured, *"What would it hurt?"* I had no idea what to expect and little did I know it was going to be the best thing that ever happened to me. I sat there and listened to the stories of the women. I was amazed at how strong and happy they were after such adversities. They had all gone through so much, and yet they were able to forgive and overcome the things they spoke about.

One specific story about forgiveness really got me thinking about my own life. I remember thinking, if this woman can go through everything she has gone through and still find forgiveness for all of those who have wronged her, then how can I not do the same? We began having a discussion amongst the people in our group; I specifically remember this question. *"Have you ever had anyone you needed to forgive and how did you go about forgiving them?"* I asked, *"How do you know you need to forgive?"* Someone replied, *"Has anyone ever hurt you, and if they have you need to tell them that you forgive them."* I thought to myself, so it's that simple ... I just tell them I forgive them. They made it seem so easy, but how could it be so easy when it seemed so hard.

When I got back to my room during a break, I was sitting all alone and I began writing down all the bad things I had been through in my life and all the people I was angry with, and all the people I had been hurt by. It all came flooding back to me as I broke down in tears.

I wrote down all the people I knew that I needed to forgive; I began saying out loud all the things I needed to forgive them for. I forgive you Michael, for molesting me as a child. I forgive you, Dad, for leaving my mom for another woman and abandoning me. I forgive you, Andrew for abusing me mentally, physically, and emotionally. I forgive you God for putting me through everything you did.

And last but not least, I forgive myself for pushing you, God, out of my life and for not allowing you to be there for me when I needed you the most and for blaming you for everything. In that moment, I literally felt a weight released from my shoulders and my heart felt at peace for the first time in 22 years.

I began to cry even harder as I finally realized that God had been there for me all along, it just wasn't in the ways that I wanted him to. I wanted God to solve all my problems and I wanted God to erase all my bad memories. I now know that I was wrong asking God to solve my problems. What God did was to give me the strength when I didn't think I had any left. He gave me the strength to walk away from that terrible relationship I was in at just the right moment.

I realized how grateful I was that God led me to this retreat. He brought me here to help me find my way back to him. I knew after that day that I was no longer going to be alone and that as long as I put my life and my heart in God's hands, he would never forsake me.
– Anonymous

Reflection: God should always be the first stop we make before we get to the point of desperation. Give thanks for everyone who played a part in your life. Thank your enemy for the lessons he taught you; thank your mother and father for the life they gave you; thank the friends that never abandoned you and thank God for always carrying you when you are most in need. – Henry Trevino

The Power of Prayer

Rejoice in your hope, be patient in tribulation, be constant in prayer. Romans 12:12

I accepted an invitation to attend an ACTS, (Adoration Community Theology Service) retreat at St Peters as a retreatant. After my first retreat as a retreatant, I was asked to serve on the ACTS team for several years. In 2016, during and after our retreat I experienced several things that inspired and strengthened me to have a stronger and deeper faith and trust in God and his word. When one serves on an ACTS retreat, as a team member, there is a lot of preparation involved. A team usually consists of about 25 or 30 women who meet at least once a week for approximately 12 weeks before the actual retreat.

During the first meeting, we were asked to pick a piece of paper from a basket. On each piece of paper was a written word and all were different. We were informed that the word we picked would have a special meaning. Our spiritual advisor guaranteed that at first, we would probably be unsure why this certain word should make any sense to us. Our advisor asked us not to worry too much about what our word meant. She said that about the end of the 12 weeks of preparation, that word would appear to us in more ways than we would think.

The word that I drew from the basket was "Prayer." It made sense to me immediately. Why? For the simple reason that I live and breathe it. I have always believed in the power of prayer and it is an important part of my daily life. It wasn't until that night when I got home, that I was sitting in my bedroom and I noticed my Bible near the nightstand. I have always had several Bibles in my house, yet it occurred to me that I never really read it on a regular basis; in fact, I couldn't remember the last time I had even picked it up. Curious, I decided to read it. No particular or special book, time of day, or in any certain order. I just began reading it randomly here and there.

One day I happened to look towards the end of the bible, where they list different topics and the books and verses in the bible that relate to each topic. So, of course I found my word "prayer" and began to read everything the bible had to say that pertained to that word. The specific verse that resonated with me was *"Rejoice in your hope, be patient in tribulation, be constant in prayer."* Romans 12:12 I repeated it constantly from that point on and even put it in my notes and on my phone so that I could constantly see it and say it in my head.

Much later in those 12 weeks of preparation for the upcoming ACTS retreat, the team members attended a mini retreat. At one point, we were asked to go outside for some quiet time alone. When we returned, everyone had a big beautiful seashell on their seats with a piece of decorative paper inside and written in gold was a bible verse. I felt my heart sink as I saw the verse, Romans 12:12. In that moment I felt the Holy Spirit come over me. Out of all the verses in the bible, that was the one picked out for me, the one that resonated with me since the beginning, the only one I had finally memorized.

Since that day, I have memorized several other verses in the Bible, but that very first one has a special place in my heart and reminds me to never cease praying. I relied on that verse again not long after that retreat.

My husband, Dain has had several life-threatening events in his lifetime. One event in particular started after a routine colonoscopy. The doctor had removed a polyp and explained to us that although that is nothing unusual; there could be a fair amount of bleeding but nothing to be concerned about.

That very next weekend, my husband and I went to our family ranch. My husband was so excited this particular trip because we were stopping at a little farm to pick up some chickens that we had already purchased. While we were driving, I noticed that my husband began to look very weak and pale. I immediately felt very uneasy and suggested that perhaps we should go back home and make the trip another time when he was feeling better. My husband is a stubborn man; he insisted it was my imagination and assured me that he felt fine.

My brother and sister-in-law joined us at the ranch and also noticed that he didn't look well. We ended up staying at the ranch for two nights, all the while with this anxious feeling in my heart. I just longed to be home. My brother and sister and their families left a few hours before us. As we were getting ready to head home, I looked at my husband again and knew without a doubt that something was terribly wrong with him. The look in his eyes this time was extremely disturbing. What I had feared this whole trip was now happening. My husband was now in desperate need of a doctor.

He was as pale as a ghost, had severely chapped lips and was very weak. Keep in mind that San Antonio is almost three hours away from our ranch in South Texas. I managed to get him in the car, and we started on our way. I was extremely apprehensive and had no idea how we were going to be on the road for three hours while he continued to look worse by the minute.

I was praying the entire way home, except when I stopped to get him some juice and a snack. I informed him that we were going straight to the hospital. To my surprise at the mention of "hospital" he became belligerent, irate and was no longer himself. I finally had to tell him that we wouldn't go straight to the hospital. I didn't want to upset him anymore, however, by this point he was lethargic, delirious and possibly losing a lot of blood. He seemed to be getting worse by the minute. I called his brother and asked him to meet us at the hospital; I was sure I was going to need his help.

We passed the town of Jourdanton, which is still an hour away from San Antonio, and as I prayed that he could just hang on a little longer, I noticed a church right off the highway. I looked at the billboard and have noticed that in the past there are usually messages about upcoming events, mass times and occasionally scriptures. On this particular day, the only thing that appeared on the sign was, Romans 12:12. I couldn't believe my eyes; yes, indeed it was exactly what I needed at that very moment. *Rejoice in your hope, be patient in tribulation, be constant in prayer.* I looked over at my husband and with a faithful heart I said, *"You are going to be ok and so am I."* I felt so relieved.

My husband was admitted to the hospital and spent five days there. After several blood transfusions, he survived. The doctors told us that it was a miracle he survived. The colonoscopy played a part in it, but there were other factors as well. I know God was with me and heard my prayer.

I will forever rely on that verse. I may have saved my husband that day, but it was I who was saved as well. Saved by the power of prayer. – *Laura Hart*

Reflections: When you are in the darkest of times, with the feeling of hopelessness and feeling completely defeated, you should turn to God in prayer. God will never forsake you. You should praise and exalt God and thank him at every opportunity for the life that he has given you. You should always accept and thank God for all your blessings and ultimately, remember that God is always in control, and with him all things are possible. – *Henry Trevino*

The Scar Left Behind

I am the Lord your God. I take hold of your right hand. I say to you, "Do not be afraid. I will help you." Isaiah 41:13

It was a balmy afternoon in the early 1990's; I was on duty at my regular fire station #16. We had just started eating when we received an emergency call from Fire Alarm. The dispatcher described the emergency as a person trapped under a tractor. On the way to the emergency, while my partner was driving, I read the notes that were transmitted by the dispatch office. I picked up the radio transmitter and told the dispatcher that this call screamed for the newly formed "RESCUE" team. The dispatchers concurred with my request and reported that the Rescue Team had been dispatched and would be on their way.

This newly formed team consisted of individuals with knowledge and specialized training to use these new specialty tools for extracting. They carried the lifesaving tool called the Hurst tool. This tool could completely dismember a car in less than five minutes. These specialized units carried many types of pneumatic extraction tools. They were invaluable, especially in car and heavy equipment crashes.

When we pulled up to the scene, which happened to be across the street from another fire station, we fully expected to have lots of help as the rescue team was coming from their home station, which was closer in proximity than our fire station. As my partner and I approached this large front loader tractor we noticed the pumper truck from that fire station parked in the middle of the street about 100 yards from the fire station and the Rescue Team was nowhere in sight.

As we fought our way through the crowd of people standing around and very close to the tractor, we saw one firefighter holding the head of a very large man that was standing chest high in the trench. Nearby was a small-framed man lying on the grass where a firefighter was tending to him. The lieutenant in charge was in the trench digging with his bare hands.

What we found out later was that the two men were digging a trench for a new sewer line. The small man was operating the tractor and the large man, weighting approximately 350 pounds, was using a shovel to clear the trench of loose dirt. The man operating the tractor did not see the man in the trench, hence he ran over him, stopping just short of decapitating him with the left wheel of the tractor. Witnesses stated that the man in the trench yelled, which caused the driver to stop the tractor. He got off; saw what he had done and fainted.

The man in the trench was conscious and barely breathing. The fire crew that was first on the scene had already placed an oxygen mask on him to maximize his ability to access oxygen with his very short labored breaths. A bystander identified herself as a nurse and took over caring for the guy on the grass. This freed three firefighters plus my partner and I, to concentrate on caring for the man in the trench.

Somehow someone realized that by putting his or her weight on the right side of the tractor it would move slightly off the man that was being crushed. While I tended to the man in the trench someone had organized bystanders to stand on the right side on the tractor. I was told later that there were probably 20 civilians either standing on the tractor or hanging on and leaning back like you would see in a sailing regatta.

I stretched my right leg into the trench, while leaving my left leg on the outside edge of the trench. I was in a very awkward and painful position. The man was resting his head on my left shoulder. I reached way down as far as I could and grabbed the man from his belt and pants while the other people began slowly rocking the tractor sideways. With each rocking motion I was able to pull the man up what seemed to be a half-inch or so. I am not sure how long this went on, but suddenly I found myself lying on my back with the man lying on top of me.

The firefighters carefully cradled his neck and rolled him over onto his back. I saw that a second EMS crew had arrived at the scene. They immediately started assisting the man that had been trapped by the tractor. Some bystanders brought a stretcher from the ambulance and placed it next to the man in the ditch.

One paramedic was tending to the driver who was now sitting but still very shaken. The other paramedic was getting all of the airway equipment needed to intubate the crushed man. Somehow, I gathered myself and was able to secure the man's airway with an endotracheal tube. We put a C-collar on him and prepared him to be transported to the hospital. We had lots of help getting him into the ambulance. I remember being pushed aside by a bystander as they carried the entire stretcher a foot off the ground to the ambulance.

Once we put the injured man in the ambulance, I continued to assist the victim while my partner drove to Brooke Army Medical Center. I was concerned with his breathing because he seemed to be gasping for air. I placed an oxygen mask on his face and provided oxygen. Once we reached the hospital, he was immediately taken into the emergency room. When we arrived at the hospital the man was conscious and was moving his fingers and toes. We noticed his eyes were bright red, which was a result from all the blood vessels bursting from the pressure exerted by the weight of the tractor on his chest. He was in dire need of help to move air in and out of his lungs.

When my partner and I reported to work the next shift we were notified that the man had died. Apparently, the damage done to his internal organs was so severe from the crushing injury that they slowly shut down. The man lived three days after arrival at the hospital.

On our next emergency trip to BAMC I spoke to a couple of people that cared for him in one of their critical care units. They told me that it was both sad and beautiful to see the man say goodbye to his wife and children knowing that his massive strong body was slowly shutting down. To this day I can still see the tears in the eyes of the nurses as they spoke to me about their time with him and his family. They were obviously a very close family. The love and respect he showed to his family was beyond description. He tried to be strong for his family through their pain and even fought taking his pain medications so that he could embrace every moment he had left.

As for me it was truly a life-changing run. Because of this experience I learned about the willingness and unselfishness of strangers willing to help others. It was humbling to witness bystanders that quickly volunteered to help with the extraction of the victim. I also learned that during times of crisis, although I can always count on God to be with me, I also could only count on first responders that are already on the scene.

It took a while to get a straight answer as to where the Rescue Team was when we really needed them. What apparently happened was that the acting Rescue Team officer was demonstrating tools and equipment to some visiting school children and their teachers. Much of their equipment was off the truck at the time the emergency was called. By the time they put their entire specialty equipment back on their apparatus, answered the alarm and arrived at the scene, all emergency crews were gone. I often wonder if the outcome would have been the same had the Rescue Team arrived in time. Would it have made a difference in the constant headaches I was experiencing that resulted from that call? It turned out that when I was pulling the man out of the ditch, I damaged three disks in my neck. This injury required attention. They placed a plate and 6 screws in order to fuse that part of my neck.

I was able to recover from my injury and return to work although I now have a large scar on the right side of my neck. It is a constant reminder of that emergency run and the resulting outcome. Each and every morning while shaving I see that permanent scar. It wasn't until several years ago I realized I often smile as I maneuver the razor blade around the scar on my neck. It now serves as a reminder that although a precious life was lost, it's comforting knowing his last days were with his loved ones by his side. I am grateful for God's help and the courage and strength he provided to all who helped on that day and allowing us, the first responders to get home safely. – *Richard Flores Ozuna*

Reflections: The past will always be a part of your life. As first responders, events happen that are out of your control. As long as you feel that you did all you could do to help someone in stress, you should be able to rest easy. – Henry Trevino)

Three Months

Lord, don't be so far away from me. You give me strength. Come quickly to help me. Psalm 22: 19

It was in the early morning hour in May 2013; my husband began nudging me to wake up. I looked at the clock and it showed 5:00 am. Out of the corner of my eye I saw my husband struggling to speak. I glanced over to see him and I knew something was wrong just by the look in his eyes. He softly whispered, *"Mary, can you please take me to the emergency room?"* I asked, *"What's the matter, Tony?"* His voice cracked as he said, *"I'm not sure, I don't feel good and I am in a lot of pain."*

Without hesitation I got up and immediately drove him to the hospital. The emergency room doctors took his vitals and gave him a CT scan. He knew that we had plans that morning to go to my granddaughter's school for an awards ceremony, where my granddaughter Sophia, was receiving the outstanding student award. Once he was stable and comfortable, he insisted that I go; the doctors had told us the testing and results were going to take a while.

As I was on my way to the school, I received a telephone call from my husband; he told me that they had completed all the tests and that they had just given him the results. *"They just told me that I have pancreatic cancer."* I immediately turned the car around and told him that I would be there as soon as possible. As I hung up the phone, I felt my heart drop to the floor, and I began crying. All I could think of, while driving with tears swelling in my eyes, was, *"This can't be happening."*

My thoughts and questions began circling in my head. *"Who told him?" "How did they know for sure," "Why didn't they wait for me to be there with him?"* Then I remembered that he had beat tongue cancer once before. I had hope now. He would beat this too.

After I picked him up from the emergency room, I drove him home and as soon as we got there, we both sat down and cried. I felt so helpless sitting there with him. I didn't know what to say to him to make him feel better, other than; we will talk to the doctor and see what he has to say. Just then the phone rang, and it was his doctor. I answered the phone and he asked me to bring my husband to his office as soon as possible.

While at the doctor's office, he confirmed that he did have cancer. He suggested that he take the chemotherapy treatment; however, the prognosis was that with chemotherapy he could possibly extend his life for three or four months at the most. He informed us that with this type of cancer the life expectancy was six to nine months, but realistically it meant three months.

My husband looked at me first and then he turned around and told the doctor, *"I don't want to do the chemo, I will have no quality of life."*

Just then my heart sank and that lump in my throat brought the tears out again. Through the tears and with shaking hands I grabbed his hand in mine and told him that I would do everything I could for him and that I would respect his decision, no matter what it was. This was when our lives changed dramatically, and it seemed as if it all changed overnight. Our routines changed from work, housekeeping, kids, friends and all that a husband and wife usually share together to a life of doctor appointments, medications, therapy, hospital beds and injections. I did what I had to do for my husband because I loved him.

But loving him did not make it easy when it came to all the questions that he began asking me. He would ask things such as, *"What do you think it will be like?" "Will I see my parents; what will happen to you when I'm gone?"* In all honesty, I did not know how to answer his questions. I realized that death and what happens after, is a true mystery. One thing I did know, and I continued to reassure him was that we would see each other again. I'm grateful that he believed that also. In fact, I don't know how people can deal with death not believing that.

The most difficult question of all was, *"Why, why me?"* He would say that he tried to be a good person all of his life, why cancer again, and why him? To this day, I don't have an answer to that question. Only God knows; God is the one who is in control of everything, we as people of faith are not supposed to question our Father or have any doubts as to why things happen the way they do. This was just so hard for me to witness though, and I still ask that question from time to time. I don't think I will ever know the answer until I make it to the other side.

My husband instructed me in what he wanted me to do. He wanted me to sell the house and all the furniture, move to an apartment and start my life over. At a time like this you are just numb, and you go along with whatever you hear. All I wanted to do was to make him comfortable. I wanted to spend every last second with him, since I did not know when the end would happen.

I think he felt the time getting closer when he would ask me to lay with him. He felt that he would soon die, and he didn't want to die alone. He would also say things such as; *"It smells like death in here, maybe the end is coming."* Attending to his every need, I even lit scented candles in every room in the house. I did not realize until much later that we could have been blown up since he was on oxygen constantly. Surely God was with us during these trying times.

Before Tony had gotten sick, we spent weekends out and about. We would hang out with friends or family and go to the movies, barbeques etc. we were very active, and it was hard adjusting to our new way of life. Our weekends now were spent crying. He felt so bad that he was not able to take me places anymore. Considering everything he was going through, it amazed me at how well he was handling his sickness yet still so concerned about my feelings.

It was by the grace of God that we both had the courage and strength to hold on to each other until the very end. Tony died three months and a few days later in September 2013. I was his constant companion, nurse, confidant, and wife until he closed his eyes for the last time.

As I look back now, I wonder if it's better to know when your life on earth is coming to an end. I don't know the answer to that, but in Tony's case I think it was better. He accepted his fate and stayed strong throughout his sickness until the very end. He had time to prepare and take care of any unfinished business. I find comfort now in the fact that I have three loving angels in heaven looking down on me: my husband, my father, and my mother. I feel their presence hovering over me telling me to stay strong and to trust and have faith in God. I think about them and pray daily to them, knowing without a doubt that one day we will be reunited for all eternity, and that is what brings me peace. – *Mary Lopez*

Reflection: What you let go is a chapter in your life that will be gone forever. So too, a loved one called by the Lord will be gone forever, however, the memories of one so loved will live in your heart for the rest of your life. – Henry Trevino

To Love, Only Like a Mother Can

She puts on strength and honor as if they were her clothes. She can laugh at the days that are coming. Proverbs 31:25

For as long as I can remember I have been surrounded by independent strong women; mothers, grandmothers, aunts, sisters, and cousins. These selfless women of matriarchy start with my own mother, Elsa, and her influence of being one hard-working mother. A natural homemaker; working outside of our home came so easy and effortless to her. It's true what they say, "a woman's work is never done." While mothering may be innate to most women, it can easily be taken for granted.

Before my family lived in the same city as our extended family, I wanted to spend quality time with my fun-loving aunts and cousins whenever I could. I had a special and unique relationship with each of my aunts. I vividly recall staying with my mom's youngest sister, Lisa, and watching her get ready for work. She would sit on the bathroom counter in a man's button down, applying her make-up while sipping her coffee. She was assertive and certainly in control of her domain.

My mom's second youngest sister, Letty, for whom I'm motivated to write this story for, also hosted me during my summers away from home. Letty is a natural caretaker. I remember how special and pampered she felt when I would give her one of my first pedicures. Caring for those I love fulfills me. My mom's sister, Laura, also holds a special place in my heart and feels like a big sister to me, more and more as I've gotten older.

My aunt Loressa's patience, grace, and loyalty have always been prominent in her personality; she influenced my personality as well. Once we moved physically closer to our extended family in San

Antonio, I continued to grow emotionally closer to the women in my family, especially my vivacious cousins. But who would these women be without the influence of their mothers?

My grandmothers also played a prominent role in my perspective of matriarchy, caretaking, and independence. The balance they orchestrated between it all, seemed so natural to them. I can't recall a time when they seemed particularly overwhelmed; but rather accepted their roles as mothers and wives.

My dad's mother, Maurice was the epitome of a "Boss Lady." Some of my fondest memories growing up were working for her over the summers at her salon, "Harts for Hair." I always enjoyed driving with her to work in her 911 Porsche, listening to NPR (National Public Radio). With great control, she adjusted the stick shift with one bedazzled hand and puffed on a cigarette with her other hand. I recount this memory often, still feeling the speed, smelling the smoke, and seeing her diamonds glisten in the sun. This moment in time and memory, converge with real life for me. The importance of balanced control became a fundamental core value for me.

My grandmother, Delia, my mom's mom, may have had a different role in her household, but her parenting to 6 children was unparalleled by anyone else in my life. She may have been more domestic than my other female role models, but she did it all with so much grace and faith in her heart. One of my favorite memories of my "Wela," which I used to call her, was watching *Three's Company* with her on the fold out couch at the "Ranch." Wela and I usually stayed up into the wee hours of the night. It felt like a special treat, having her company to myself and staying up late. The next day, I wanted to treat her and recall combing her hair and putting make-up on her. She was such a sweet selfless woman, even after her stroke, always just going with the flow. She was the best example of acceptance and optimism, no matter her own restrictions or handicaps.

Fast-forward to my blossoming adulthood and my upbringing, which would eventually bring shape to my life's journey. My own entrepreneurship came to fruition in the way of "Flirt Boutique" and now a skin line called "HartYourSkin." When I think of the outpouring of love and support that has always surrounded me; unconditional loves come to mind. I had the courage and confidence that it took to be a risk taker and go against the norm; the norm of a full time, corporate job. My parents were traditionalists after all; their security served our family well. No matter where my myriad of job opportunities took me, or my romantic relationships gained or lost, my family supported my decisions.

Now as a mother myself, I see more than ever, the value of maintaining balance in all aspects of life. Taking the life lessons I've learned from all the great "Mother's" and women in my life and invoking their strength and fortitude to guide me. I treasure our many happy memories and appreciate these dynamic women so much. I hope they know how much they have shaped the spirited woman and mother I am today.

I have such deep respect for all that they have endured through life, through death, through sickness, and through health. These women that have been there through it all, prevailed and triumphed, especially when life felt out of control. They continue to carry on with love, courage, forgiveness, and faith in their hearts. I may not have a baby girl of my own and see a daughter grow to be a mother, but I will forever know what it feels like to love ... to love only like a mother can. – *Melissa Hart*

Reflection: Mothers are the ones that give you life, they give you wisdom, knowledge and they give you love. Mother's are like children, always forgiving and forgetting. They don't hold grudges against their loved ones. Mothers are happy when their children succeed. The love and compassion of a mother can never be equated by anyone else. – Henry Trevino)

Two Loves To Remember – Two Great Women

Trust in the Lord with all your heart. Do not depend on your own understanding. Proverbs- 3:5

    My first love, my wife Martha (Marty) died in 1983. She marched off to her final resting place leaving her family of five children and her husband. She was 48 years old when she passed away. We had been married for 32 years. Our youngest son was nine years old at the time of her passing. The first two years after her death were the hardest time I have ever experienced. I roamed around in a fog for months. My weight was affected tremendously. I lost all desire to eat; I had no appetite. I lost 35 lbs. in 30 days.

    I lived by myself for about twelve years with no direction of what to do or where to go. During my 12 years of single status, some relationships entered my door and then faded with the passing of time. It seemed that there was never a right fit for a long-term commitment. It was hard coming into my empty home every day. The most difficult time of the day was after 6 pm. When darkness fell and the world felt silent, loneliness weighed heavy on my shoulders.

    It was not until the year 1992 that my life started to change. Two very close friends of mine wanted to introduce me to a lady who had lost her husband a few years past. I had gone through this scenario many times before and I knew full well that permanency was probably not going to be in this introduction.

    My friends told me that the lady they wanted me to date was interested in meeting me. Actually, I later learned that the lady did not want to meet me, and she also had reservations about who I was. The insistence of my two friends kept up for a couple of months. We finally agreed to meet and see what would happen. We went to dinner with our two friends and then went dancing that evening.

Well lo and behold; the lady, Mary Lou, was the sister of one of my best friends. Her brother, Ralph, and I had been friends since we were sixteen or seventeen years old; in fact, her brother was in my first wedding. I visited Ralph at his home often; however, I never remember meeting his sister, Mary Lou.

Mary Lou, then a girl, and I were both in a 15-year *Quinceanera*. The traditional *Quinceanera* is a Spanish word given to a celebration for a girl coming-of-age on her 15th birthday. It was a celebration for a girl that we both knew. The young debutant had her escort. Additionally, there were 15 couples accompanying the debutant and her escort. Mary Lou had her escort and I escorted another girl. Later in our relationship, Mary Lou showed me a picture of the debutant celebration and sure enough, we were both in the picture.

Mary Lou mentioned my name to her brother; immediately he knew who I was. Upon his insistence she agreed to meet me. I understand that he told her that I was a good man and that we would have a lot of fun; but he said, tongue in cheek, just in case, take a quarter with you in case you have to make a telephone call.

The rest is history. We married and lived a very good life together for twenty-two years. We bought a town house in San Antonio and also a condo in Corpus Christi. We lived in both places and made some beautiful friendships in the course of our relationship. We traveled to many Mexico cities, went on several cruises, parties, get-to-gathers were every weekend. All holidays were always celebrated with a lot of fun and a lot of friends.

Mary Lou had one young son still living with her and I had my young son still living with me. Eventually both the boys got married and left the nest. There was never a day that one of our kids didn't call to say hello or to see how we were. Between the two families we had a total of nine kids; there were seven boys and two girls.

I retired from the Fire Department in 1996. As the storybook goes; "we lived happily ever after." We spent many happy years together with our children and our friends. Our marriage filled a great void left with the death of my first wife.

One night on February 14, 2014 I went to bed around 10p.m. Mary Lou always stayed up to see the news and would come to bed thirty minutes later. I was reading a book in bed while she went into the rest room to shower and dress for bed. When she came out of the rest room she sat at the end of the bed. She was still for a few moments. All of sudden I heard her say in a loud voice; "*Henry, Henry, I can't feel my left arm and my left leg.*" I immediately got up and walked her to the dining room where we had a blood pressure monitor. I tried to get her blood pressure several times, but the monitor kept indicating, error, and error.

I walked her back to the bed and sat her down. She became very lethargic, slurring her words and unable to move her limbs. While helping her dress I noticed her bottom lip start to fall to one side. It was a classic sign that my wife was having a major stroke. I called EMS and gave them my address and the possibility that my wife was having a stroke. The fire station is about one mile from my house. I heard the siren of the ambulance and the fire truck before I hung up the phone. The First Responders were at our house in five minutes or less.

My wife was loaded onto the ambulance and immediately rushed to the hospital. Before the ambulance left, I told the paramedics that I would follow. I was going to close the house and take a list of her medications to give to her doctors. I got to the hospital a few minutes after the ambulance arrived.

Arriving at the hospital I was immediately met by a doctor and some paramedics. The doctor asked me to sit down. I told her I was o.k. The doctor insisted that I sit down. I refused and insisted that the doctor tell me the condition of my wife. The doctor said, *"How far do you want us to go with this?"*

I asked the doctor for more details and what she was alluding to. *"We are preforming CPR at this time and inserting a tube in her trachea, (windpipe) to enable her to breath."* The doctor said: *"If she continues to live, she will not have a functional life." "What do you want us to do?"* I told the doctor that she had a DNR, (do not resuscitate) request in her files. I requested that all medical procedures continue at least until some of Mary Lou's children arrived at the hospital. I could not consciously make the final decision without support from her children.

Before the ambulance left our house I told my sister-in-law, who lived next to our house, to call Mary Lou's children and ask them to come to the hospital immediately. At the hospital, Mary Lou's children started to arrive. Some of my children also came to the emergency room. Mary Lou's sister, Virginia, also came to the hospital. Mary Lou's children agreed on ceasing all lifesaving procedures. The doctor and his team stopped all medical procedures.

We all entered the room that Mary Lou was in and said our last goodbyes. Mary Lou, my dear wife, quietly passed into the arms of our Lord. It was hard for us to leave the hospital and not take Mary Lou with us; in fact, as we were walking out of the hospital I stopped and told the kids, *"Let me go get my wife."*

I went home to a lonely, dark and cold house. My mind wondered back years to the time I lost my first wife, the mother of our five children. The day I took her to the hospital she died as soon as she arrived. I didn't even get a chance to say goodbye. Her death was caused by a large tumor in her head that had never been diagnosed.

My dear second wife also died as soon as she arrived at the hospital. An aneurism in her head had burst and covered her brain with blood. The doctor showed me her x-rays. I will never forget that moment in time.

I have lost two beautiful and faithful women in my life. I saw different beauties in each of my wives. Each had different characteristics, different moods and dispositions; what they had in common was loyalty, faithfulness, beauty, friendliness, and devotion to the families, religion and most important was their love they shared with me and accepting my love for them.

It has been years since their passing, but I still remember and pray for them every day. I see our children and they remind me very much of their mothers. I can truthfully say that I have lived a very joyful life with two beautiful women who were my faithful friends and companions. – *Henry Trevino*

Reflections: Those we love don't go away; they walk beside us every day. They are unseen and unheard but always very close. Our loved ones go away but their legacy stays with us forever. Their memories, their love and their friendship will continue to inspire us everyday. They will forever be by our side. In this life we will miss them deeply, but we can reminisce and appreciate the many memories made by our loved ones. – Henry Trevino

Weeds to Wildflowers – Lessons in Life and Love

"There is a time for everything, and a season for every activity under the heavens." Ecclesiastes 3:1

Being a seventeen-year-old girl in a small town can be an interesting and enlightening experience. Thirty years ago, I was that girl. I learned a lot about how powerful and influential adults could be in the lives of teenagers. The adults in my life were as varied and riveting as a garden full of spring flowers. Some would definitely be considered blooms that would be better off in a hothouse.

Other flowers were tough and beautiful, their bright faces always turned towards the warmth of the sun. Some could be called perennials, always there, year after year while others were more fleeting like the rain lilies that show up in my yard after a violent spring cloudburst. A few would definitely be classified as weeds. I learned something valuable from each one; lessons that were hard, surprising, and beautiful. Lessons that even today still remind me of the young girl I was and the strong woman I have become.

Bluebonnets remind me of my civics teacher, Mrs. Lockman. She had very long dark hair, worn straight, loose, and parted down the middle. I could tell she let her hair dry naturally because of the gentle waves that did not look quite brushed out. She was at least forty years old, but she carried herself as if she was a ravishing, sensual, twenty-something-beauty that everyone's eyes should follow. Everyone's eyes *did* follow her in class. She wasn't especially attractive, but the way she moved made you think she was. She tossed that long hair around as if it was the most luxurious mane that ever existed.

Bluebonnets aren't especially pretty flowers, but in Texas, they are special. They draw your attention wherever they happen to pop up. Mrs. Lockman taught me that beauty is not about the package. Beauty is an attitude, a way of thinking, a way of moving through the world with grace and confident trust.

Every Easter my grandmother, who lived in Michigan, would send me seed packets of forget-me-nots. In Texas, forget-me-nots, are perennial and invasive, they are almost considered weeds. In Michigan though, they are annuals, and they're quite a prized addition to any northern garden. I loved my grandmother so much and I didn't want to hurt her feelings by throwing them away, so over the years I had accumulated quite a collection. I never planted those seeds until I was a wife and mother.

I did not understand the pleasure of helping things grow until I had children and a home of my own. As a teenager, I would visit "Granna" every summer. She never failed to make me feel loved and appreciated. Every picture I drew, every song I sang, anything I did, regardless of its insignificance to the rest of the world, was special in the eyes of Granna. Whether she was on her knees in her bedroom, fingering her rosary beads, or huffing around in her kitchen making blueberry cobbler, she could do no wrong. To me, she was the best woman on the planet. Granna planted seeds in my heart that to this day are perennially with me. I believe in a sense of pride for a job well done, faith, no matter how tough things can be, laugh when things seem to be hopeless and to love, no matter what. When I see forget-me-nots, I remember visiting my Granna in my seventeenth summer and wishing I didn't have to go home. Granna taught me there are blessings even in the ugliest of situations.

When I was seventeen, I was very involved in athletics, so my coaches played a big part in my life. My track coach, Mr. Bushwitz, always had a smile on his face. No matter how angry my teammates and I could make him with our less-than-stellar efforts, he was a very tough coach. If he felt we were not trying hard enough, he would swear like a sailor at us. He was gruff, loud and demanding, but only for so long. I always knew that at some point during practice or track meets his tough face would break out into an exasperated smile; he just couldn't help himself. We were so bad by trying to make him angry. Eventually, he would just laugh and then swear at us some more.

He was the kind of man that I would never have gone up to for a hug or outright asked him for encouragement. That just wouldn't have felt right. It wasn't because I was afraid to approach him; it was because we were able to appreciate the value in each other from a short distance. It seemed that he was just too bright and strong to get too physically close to. There was nothing better than seeing the look of pride in his eyes when he thought we had run a good race. Those occasions were rare, but they stayed with us and kept us trying our best to please him.

When I was seventeen, Mr. Bushwitz had a heart attack. We were shocked. The world stopped and there was utter silence in the stadium for days. Practices were canceled and track meets rescheduled. Mr. Bushwitz eventually recovered, but he never could coach again. He would get too worked up and it was not good for his heart. The track team that remained was never the same; our inspiration was gone. Coach Bushwitz would definitely be a marigold. A bright, simple flower with a strong medicinal smell that puts you off if you get too close; it would make you think it doesn't *want* you to get too close. Marigolds always burn very brightly despite the hot Texas sun. Their apparent strength and beauty could make you forget their vulnerability. Mr. Bushwitz taught me never to take talent for granted. He always maintained that underused and underappreciated talents and gifts could be taken away when we least expected it.

Being part of the yearbook staff was a big deal in those days, although it was not easy to be selected. One had to get the approval of Mr. Cline who was the sponsor of the yearbook. He was a very high-strung, creative man. I knew I would have to wipe off any hint of sarcasm or insincerity from my face during my "pre-approval" interview. People constantly made fun of him. He could be prissy and emotional as well as a bit paranoid. He had a habit of throwing up his hands in a very feminine way any time he didn't like something. I knew it was just because he was a perfectionist and he was impatient with half-hearted efforts. I understood this; I had grown up with a mother that was just like him.

Mr. Cline would be a violet, truth be-told, fragile and full of promise. However, his fragility prevented him from realizing his full potential. He was too delicate for our imperfect world to foster his growth. I think I understood the underlying frustration that he had so much difficulty controlling because it underlined everything my mother did to me in my young life. It felt familiar. In any case, Mr. Cline accepted my request to be on the yearbook staff and it was one of the best experiences I ever had. Mr. Cline taught me that it was easy to overlook what a person has to offer when emotions get in the way. It's easy to just write people off when their prickly-pear behavior can prevent you from seeing their potential. When I think of Mr. Cline, I am reminded to handle people gently no matter how violently they might enter my life or how much bluster they may exhibit. By being gentle I can remain quiet and focused. I can see their light and be inspired.

I was a pretty seventeen-year-old girl, tall and thin, muscled, with blond hair and green eyes. As a teenager I did not fully understand what physical beauty could do. I really didn't understand that I *WAS* attractive or what being attractive meant. Enter Mr. Callaway, our Vice Principal. At seventeen, I was basically a good kid, not just an athlete, but also a straight A student. I belonged to a few school organizations in leadership positions and obeyed the rules most of the time; oh, I drank a few beers, back when the drinking age was eighteen and smoked a few cigarettes once in a while. Mr. Callaway never had any problems with me.

One night at a particularly heated basketball game, I lost my temper beyond what was socially acceptable. During half time on the way to the locker room I flipped-off an opposing team player who had been very aggressive with me in the game. One of the town busybodies, Lois Potter, was in the audience that night and saw me do it, though no one else had seen me do the flipping. The next day, a bunch of my friends and I went to the local Pizza Inn for lunch. A few of my eighteen-year-old friends ordered a pitcher of beer to wash down the pizza and salad we were all having. I had another game that evening, so I was not going to sneak any beer, though I thought about it. Unbeknownst to me, Ms. Lois Potter and her tall, white, heavily sprayed beehive hair were also at the Pizza Inn. She saw us with the beer and assumed that I was also drinking. She couldn't stand that I was drinking beer. She had to call the school and report me for the beer and the bad behavior from the night before.

After lunch, Mr. Callaway called me to the office. I was a little nervous, but I didn't think too much about it. That was until I saw a few of my friends from lunch walking out from his office. They had very sheepish looks on their faces so then I became worried. Mr. Callaway and our school Principal, Mr. Brooms, were waiting for me in the outer room. They both smiled at me. Mr. Callaway blushed when I met his gaze, as we walked into Mr. Brooms' office. I felt a curious sense of relief, and then I felt what could only be described as a power that began to fill my body.

Mr. Brooms was very nice as he questioned me about the incident the night before and the beer drinking at lunch. I felt Mr. Callaway was trying not to respond to my voice or my physical presence while Mr. Brooms kept speaking. Mr. Brooms continued reminding me of the leadership responsibilities I had as a member of the school athletic program. When Mr. Brooms was finished speaking, I looked hard at Mr. Callaway, right in his eyes again, and again he blushed, as I walked away. To this day, I don't remember much of what Mr. Brooms said to me, or the consequences caused by my behavior. I can vividly recall the physical sensations that I felt in the room. Mr. Brooms' protective and professional wall against my femininity and Mr. Callaway's' inability to hide his attraction to it.

Mr. Callaway could only be a rose. A rose bud has some color, but it's still tightly wound up with green fronds of unbroken protective covering. As it begins to bloom and the color of the flower begins to spread like a blush on its petals, the blooming rose promises fragrant, thorny, beauty and strength that are not immediately apparent to the world. In full bloom, few would argue that there is no flower more beautiful than a rose. However, its beauty is temporary, fading almost as quickly as it reaches its summit. The memory of the rose in bloom is what lasts, not the flower itself. Mr. Callaway taught me that being a woman is a powerful responsibility that must be used with deliberate and honest intention to leave goodness in the world.

I played the flute in our school band and was pretty good at it when I applied myself. The band director, Mr. Solemon, was quite a colorful character. He was the person who taught me how to play a musical instrument. By the time I was seventeen, I really enjoyed playing the flute and being part of the band. Mr. Solemon had become a friend.

My life up until age seventeen had been pretty turbulent. I had a violent alcoholic father who divorced my mother when I was fifteen. He finally got tired of terrorizing us and decided to move on to greener pastures. Mr. Solemon was one of those "lights" I like to call them; those teachers that somehow on some level know your situation at home even though you never tell them. The "lights" keep you going, give you something you are not getting at home. He gave love very discreetly and gently in a way that you could appreciate receiving it.

Mr. Solemon made me laugh and helped me to feel like I belonged even though a lot of times I felt like an alien. What I didn't know at the time was that he was also struggling. In my youthful selfishness, I didn't appreciate his kindness more deeply. People, who are suffering are sometimes the ones that have the most compassion for the suffering of others. Mr. Solemon had made some decisions about his wife and family and another woman. The situation with the other woman that lived in the town blew up his family and the woman's family. It was not solely the fault of Mr. Solemon; the woman was also a willing participant in the debacle. Unfortunately, his status in the town was greatly diminished. He looked sad all of the time. I still admired him, though, and I always pretended that I didn't know what happened.

I treated Mr. Solemon the same way I always had. He was still my friend and I still sought him out when I needed reassurance, however I was never honest about the need of reassurance with him. But he knew what I needed, and he gave it to me despite whatever tempest was raging in his world. Just like one of those rain lilies that pops up the next morning amidst all the fallen tree limbs and blown leaves after a strong spring storm,

He was always there, standing straight and tall, bouncing with the rhythm of the music we were playing, while he waved his baton from the dais. I understood from him that grief and disaster doesn't have to stop you from living a good and useful life, you can still have moments of joy, despite difficulties and pain. He taught me that you have to keep going, no matter what's happened, no matter how tough the situation. He helped me to understand that there was still a place for me in this world even if I'm not what everyone thinks I should be.

Another one of those teacher-lights that taught me a lesson was Mrs. Klovak. She was a tall, very fair, dark-haired woman who always had a somewhat startled-looking expression on her face. She was my English teacher and English was my best subject. One of the roles I played in school was the class clown. I was not a physically comedic clown, but rather a verbally sarcastic clown. For whatever reason, all of my teachers put up with it, including Mrs. Klovak. One day, in her class I was feeling pretty cocky. Our basketball team had won a big championship and we were going to a play-off game that night to take an even bigger win. On game days we all wore our letter jackets whether it was cold or not. So, there I am, in my letter jacket sitting in the front of the room and I'm making my usual smart-mouth comments periodically to the annoyance of Mrs. Klovak.

The kids kept laughing every time I popped off and she began to get a flush in her face. I could see that she was getting angry, but of course I don't shut my mouth. Finally, we are at a standoff, she's had it with my comments and she warns me that if there is one more comment, she will send me to the Principal's office. I could tell that she didn't want to do it. So, what do I do? I test her. I pop off again and she says to me with a tight smile, *"That's it, Terri; time to go."* I just looked at her, stunned, wanting to take it back, but knowing it's too late. I was embarrassed beyond belief. She was embarrassed, too. I could see it on her face that she wished it hadn't come to this.

Our relationship was changed forever because of words we both said that were stupid and senseless. Daisies, especially white ones, are bright and startling to look at. White daisies don't have a fragrance, but nevertheless your eye is drawn to them because in a garden they have a special presence. You appreciate that they are there because they are rather difficult to grow, especially in Texas. If you find them in a Texas garden it's a surprise, a transplant of sorts. But once there, they are tough and will come back each year with the right cultivation.

Mrs. Klovak was certainly a daisy. She was there for me many times in my seventeenth year. She cultivated my writing skills and encouraged me. She taught me that words have power. Words create energy and space for that energy created once they are spoken. They cannot be taken back, and they cannot be erased from memory. Words can change things forever so they must be spoken with thought and care. As I look back now, I realize how much she tolerated my not so nice behavior and how much I took that for granted.

Now I must address the weeds. There are always weeds in any fine garden no matter how well the garden is cared for. The weeds in my seventeenth year would be the adults in that small town that separated themselves from the rest of the community because of their wealth and "status". Those adults will remain nameless; however, they knew who they were.

In this small town there were maybe, ten or twelve families that considered themselves to be above the rest of us because of the wealth they had accumulated. Never mind that they were nothing more than big fish in a small pond. To a seventeen-year-old girl that had grown up in a middle-class family and a tight budget, these weeds and their wealth were very intimidating. The weeds were nice to me because I played sports well and was in the local paper a lot. This gave me some notoriety, but they didn't want me to date their sons; I wasn't good enough.

They never told me to my face, I was just supposed to figure that out by myself. Their sons were happy to come over to my house and see me, but they could never take me to their homes to spend time with them. I was good enough to kiss in the back seat of a car or on my front porch, but not good enough to take to a family gathering or dance at a place where their parents were. It bothered me, but it didn't stop me from seeing those sons of weeds.

Wealth and status were never things that I dreamed about. I dreamed about being a rock star. I dreamed about playing basketball when I went to college. My dreams were about achievement, about seeing the world, being whatever I thought I could be. Dating the sons of weeds was just part of my young life and nothing more than that. I eventually fell hard for one of those boys and allowed him to become the focus of my life for a while. This relationship caused me to have a different life than the one my seventeen-year-old mind had originally dreamed of.

The weeds in that small town taught me that wealth gives you access. However, it could not give you the love and wisdom necessary to enjoy the good things that wealth can bring to the person who understands its purpose. Like physical beauty, wealth can be fleeting. It can be taken away at any moment. What you have left is what is in your heart, which is what really matters.

This strong woman wishes she could have been there for the seventeen-year-old girl she was. Maybe she would have made different choices. Certainly, she would have had a different life. But would it have been better? Would that seventeen-year-old girl have paid any attention to the lessons and the wisdom a strong woman had to share? That is the question. I like to think that maybe this seventeen-year-old girl would have listened, perhaps even considered the strong woman's advice. In the end, however, she most likely would still make the same choices and follow the path that she was being called to follow. Every garden must allow its God-given seeds to bloom. – *Terri Edgington*

Reflection: One should never let the past dictate who you are; you should just let your past be a part of who you'll become. The links that you have created in your young and formidable life such as family, friends, relationships, interactions and associations are what have made you what you are today. – Henry Trevino

Unwanted

Very truly I tell you, you will weep and mourn while the world rejoices. You will grieve, but your grief will turn to joy. John 16:20

    I never knew my mother; the judge found my mother to be an unfit mother. The gavel sounded and I was awarded to my dad. My father came back from the war and found out that my mother had a baby from another man. My parents divorced because of the infidelity of my mom. After the divorce my father and I lived with different family members or close friends that my dad knew. One experience that I had was when I had to sleep with a lady that was quite sadistic; she would pinch and twist my skin, which caused a burning pain. This caused me to have perpetual bruises.

    I was eventually moved to a cot against a bedroom wall. There was a belt hanging on the wall, which was used by my dad whenever he thought I should be punished. One time when he was whipping me the pain was so severe that it made me urinate. My dad was so infuriated that it caused him to whip much harder. I now wonder what I had done to make my dad so angry; I was only a child. The beatings continued until I was 19 years old.

    My dad eventually married a lady that I got to know as my mom. One day she told me that my dad beat me so much because I looked like my real mom. I remember when my dad took me to meet my future stepmom; she was in bed with her sister Mickie. My dad said, *"This is Vera."* The lady with a smile lifted her hand and waved and said, *"Hi, Vera."* I turned and hugged my dad's leg; that was how old I was. My stepmom had a three-year-old daughter, Lupe, from a previous marriage. I quickly learned to refer to my stepmom as my mother; she was the only mother I ever knew. My stepmom and dad added four girls to the family. My stepmom told my dad very clearly at the beginning of their relationship; *"You discipline your daughter and I will discipline my daughters."* My dad continued to use the belt on me frequently, however I never knew why. My mom often told me that I reminded him of what she had done to him. My mom would dress me with long sleeves and long pants and tell me not to let the teacher see the belt slashes and marks because they would take my father away.

One day we were driving on a city street. I was standing on the floor of the back seats. I was about six years old. I saw a building and blurted out, *"That's where my mother lives."* My father stopped the car and told me to get out of the car and go look for my mother. I started to cry; he slammed the back door and got back in the car and started driving again.

As I grew older my dad would slap me across the face; one time he slapped me so hard that the force threw me against the wall and caused my nose to bleed. I went to the bathroom and wiped my face with a towel; again, I thought, *'What did I do, why did he slap me?'* At one time my mom tried to intervene and stop my dad from beating me! He glared viciously at her and shouted, *"Get away from here."* He scared my mom and she never interfered again. She never knew how severe the beating would get. He left the room and let my mom help me to stop the bleeding and clean up the mess.

I remember that my stepsister needed orthopedic shoes. My dad thought that I should also wear orthopedic shoes. I was already in high school and I hated to wear those shoes; I always preferred to wear my ballerina shoes. When I went out the door, I would be wearing my orthopedic shoes. As soon as I left the house, I would take them off and hide them in the bushes and changed to my ballerina shoes. One day after school my orthopedic shoes were not in the bushes. My dad asked me where my shoes were. I told him I didn't know; immediately I knew I was in trouble. My dad grabbed me by my hair and threw me to the floor. He kept banging my forehead on the floor. I could see the orthopedic shoes under the bed. After the beating I knew that I would never again wear my ballerina shoes.

One day I was playing with my little sister, Lupe. We were running around the house and laughing. Dad slammed his fist on the top of my head with such force that my eyes rolled back and my body went limp. He caught me by the shoulders and yelled at me and shouted, *"That's why I don't want you running in the house!"* Him holding me by the shoulders was the closest hug I ever got from my father.

When I was nineteen, Dad came and faced me real close, nose-to-nose and told me, *"I want you out of this house."* I could see the hate in his eyes. I thought to myself; *'Why does he have such hate for me?'* He had a way of saying, *"If you don't like the way I treat you, there's the street waiting for you."* If I didn't wash the dishes the right way or I didn't make up the beds correctly, I was punished. Once I didn't cook the peas long enough to make them tender. For punishment all I had to eat was peas for breakfast, lunch and supper.

I never thought that when he said, *'There's the street,"* that he meant it. I thought to myself, *'What father would throw his daughter out on the street?'* Well, the day came when he faced me and told me **"There's the street,"** and that was when I knew that he really meant it. I had gotten a job at Montgomery Wards and made friends with Evelyn. She was simple unassuming little girl who had a small apartment. I asked her if I could move in with her and share the rent. Evelyn was all for it. I had finally found my freedom.

I never hated my father. I never wished anything wrong would befall my dad. Really, what I wanted was to die. I wanted my dad to see me in the coffin and he could say to himself, *"Why didn't I treat her better?"* I often think back to my days with my dad, I would say to myself; *"It's too bad that my father never loved me, I was a good child, I helped with all the chores in the house. Sometimes I had to stay home from school so I could baby-sit my younger sisters."* I was a good person, but I was never appreciated,

I used to hold onto the kitchen table real hard and say; *"Lord, as my penance, I offer the sacrifice that I suffered in my young life. Many times, I felt forsaken by you. I got to the point that I believed that you also wanted me to suffer. Now I realize that you never left myside. During my time of suffering I read the story, <u>Two Feet in the Sand</u>."* That story opened my eyes and I realized that God had always been by my side. *"You allowed me to finish my education, I became a nurse, I bought and paid for a small house, I have a small car and now I'm the happiest person in the world."*

Thank you, dear Lord, for everything that you have given me; without your blessings I could not have survived. Thank you for always being at my side during my darkest hours. The only good thing I can say about my father is that he always made sure that we had food, however simple, on the table. On day at supper, I said jokingly, *"Rice and beans again."* My father said; *"It's food—eat it."*

I'm writing my story now, but I don't think about the past. I survived the many years of extreme sacrifice, but to me it's history—let history rest. Thinking too much about the past brings it to the present. I was hurt mentally and physically; why hurt myself anew. This has been my life; now I aim for happiness and I alone am responsible for my own happiness; no other person is going to give it to me. Amen. – *Vera*

Reflections: You can say, *"I lived my young years with constant fear of what would happen in the next two minutes." Yes, I suffered tremendously but I grew up to be a strong and a determined woman. Now I know that I can recover and adapt to whatever adversity comes along. One should never allow oneself to erase one day of your life; the good days give you happiness; the bad days give you strength and the worst days show you how to live and survive. – Henry Trevino*

Epilog

The compilation of this book of short stories is a combination of events in the lives of every day, average and ordinary people. Most of the stories come from people that wanted to share their tragedies, misfortunes, successes and sometimes-personal triumphs. These stories do not follow a pattern, subject, theme or focus. They are random and unconnected accounts of personal problems or successes one from the other.

The authors of these stories wanted other people to know that they were not alone when misfortunes came their way. They wanted their friends to know that there was help available to them. These authors learned that personal energy and perseverance helped them surmount the many life and death problems that are faced every day. They wanted their friends to fight and maintain a determination and never allow themselves to give up.

Some of the stories are not all doom and gloom; some of the stories have happy endings. We give credit to the writers that have hit adversity head on. With great determination and tenacity they have conquered their inner most fears and as a result found resolution and happiness to their life stories.

Some of the experiences of these writers were heart wrenching, and at times the events came to a very tragic finish. It took friendly and loving coaching to persuade many of the writers to tell their stories. Some did not want to resurrect long past hurts and sad endings to their experiences.

I sat with some of the authors while they were writing their stories. I could see the worry and remembrance of their events in the eyes of the writers. Many eventually burst into tears while they were telling their life story.

We sincerely hope that in a small way these stories will help you prevail and overcome some of the everyday stressful events. Remember, the important thing is never to give up. We can assume that your friends and neighbors are probably suffering similar grief and misery. Tell your story and seek help and assure yourself that you are not alone and by so doing you could be helping someone that is suffering with heart wrenching events

Henry Trevino

www.ingramcontent.com/pod-product-compliance
Lightning Source LLC
Chambersburg PA
CBHW051755040426
42446CB00007B/384